THE LONDON G

CW00927353

Fleet Street, Holborn & the Inns of Court

COVER PHOTOS

Front: The Royal Courts of Justice
Inside front: 'Old Holborn'
Inside back: The Public Records Office

FRONTISPIECE

Middle Temple Lane through the encrusted arch
of Temple Gardens Building

DRIVE SLOWLY

THE LONDON GUIDES

Fleet Street, Holborn & the Inns of Court

ROGER HUDSON

Photographs by
JOE WHITLOCK BLUNDELL

HAGGERSTON PRESS

© Text: Roger Hudson, 1995
© Photographs: Joe Whitlock Blundell, 1995

First published in 1995
by The Haggerston Press,
38 Kensington Place, London w8 7PR
Unauthorised duplication contravenes
applicable laws

Printed in Great Britain
at The Bath Press, Avon

A CIP record is available from the British Library

1—869812—12—3

CONTENTS

Roger Hudson has lived in London for thirty years, editing other people's books for most of them. He has also compiled and edited a number of books for the Folio Society in the last six.

Joe Whitlock Blundell is a photographer and book designer. He has had three one-man shows in London and one at the Royal Photographic Society in Bath. His book *Westminster Abbey – The Monuments* was published in 1989.

MAPS

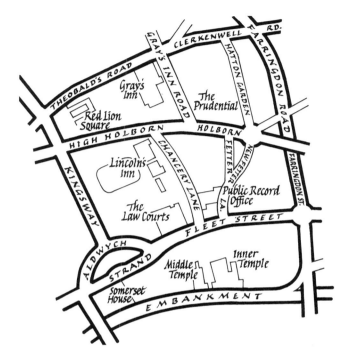

Detailed maps appear on the following pages:

PREFACE

The writers of guidebooks to the whole of London suffer from a disadvantage: the place is too big. In order to cover its great stretches they are always hurrying on, before they have done justice to a district. There are many people who would like more than they get from the existing guides: those who live and work in a particular district; Londoners from other areas who know the pleasure to be got from a closer acquaintance with an unfamiliar bit of the Capital; and wise tourists who don't attempt too much, but instead concentrate on one or two of the most interesting parts of London.

The area of legal London covered in this book, with its high density of good buildings and literary and historic associations, has particular claims to more detailed treatment. The book's boundaries are Theobald's Road to the North, the Thames to the South, Kingsway and the Aldwych to the West, and Farringdon Street and New Bridge Street to the East. So it is a mix of City, Camden and Westminster. It is structured in the form of four walks, but how literally they are adhered to is a question of personal taste and endurance. The walks can of course start at any place or end at any point along their length. If only the Inns themselves are wanted, that is an easy matter because from Gray's to Lincoln's, and from Lincoln's to the Temple is a couple of minutes' walk in each case.

Apart from the users already suggested above, it is hoped that members of the legal profession of this and other countries will also find the guide helpful. They must forgive the piece at the end of the book about the origins and collective history of the Inns and their members, what the various ranks and types of lawyers were or are, and how matters are shaping in their profession at present. It is aimed at the ordinary reader without a legal background.

This is perhaps the place to touch on one aspect that hasn't been given its due in what follows: people-watching. Look out for such comparatively new phenomena as the clusters of furtive smokers outside offices with a no-tobacco policy, or the lunchtime joggers setting out to punish themselves along the Embankment. Look into sets of chambers at the secretaries untying the bundles of papers relating to a particular case, still held together with pink tape although there are PCs in each corner of the room. Notice the apparently infinite variations on the black suit worn by the many women within the legal profession; the barristers in peculiar cut-down jackets or waistcoats, wearing white bands, on their way to the Law Courts; the City policemen with their ribbed helmets.

This also seems a fitting place to mourn those distinguished buildings to which you cannot be guided because they were pulled down earlier this century. There was the Birkbeck Bank by Thomas E. Knightley in High Holborn at the top of Chancery Lane, called in Pevsner (*The Buildings of England: London I*) 'a phantasmagoria in Doulton's majolica' and demolished in 1965; then Alfred Waterhouse's 'prodigious' red-brick and terracotta New Court in Carey Street demolished in 1964. Off Fleet Street, Racquet Court went in the 1970s, and Clifford's Inn in 1934. In Fleet Street Praed's Bank by Sir John Soane went in 1923, whilst Norman Shaw's Edwardian Baroque Gaiety Theatre at the western end of the Aldwych island succumbed in 1955, in spite of what its chorus line had done to reinvigorate various aristocratic bloodlines. The Stoll Theatre at the south-east end of Kingsway went in 1960. Bertie Crewe built it in 1911 for Oscar Hammerstein I as a rival to Covent Garden. The Duke of Norfolk's estate around Surrey Street and Arundel Street south of the Strand lost nearly all its Victorian buildings in about 1970. Lastly, J. L. Pearson's Gothic church of St John's, Red Lion Square, was bombed in the Blitz.

We would like to thank the following for helping the genesis of this book in many different ways: Jane Armstrong, Nicholas Cooper, Charles Foster, Elizabeth Gillespie, Sarah Hudson, John Naylor, Liz Robinson, Lord Roskill, and David Eccles, who drew the maps. Those who wish to pursue further the history of the Inns of Court should turn to the following titles, which have been of great assistance when writing pages 113 to 123 of this book: *The Inns of Court under Elizabeth I and the Early Stuarts*, Wilfrid R. Prest, 1972; *Gentlemen and Barristers: The Inns of Court and the English Bar 1680-1730*, David Lemmings, 1990; *The English and Colonial Bars in the Nineteenth Century*, Daniel Duman, 1983.

WALK ONE

Gray's Inn and Holborn to the Viaduct

At the traffic lights outside the Holborn tube station, cross High Holborn and head north a short way up Southampton Row. In the middle of the road tram lines go down a ramp and then disappear into the barred entry arch of a tunnel, for this was the start of the **Kingsway Tram Subway**, opened in 1906 and finally closed in 1952. Its southern part was turned into the Strand underpass for motor traffic in 1964, starting at Waterloo Bridge and emerging halfway up Kingsway, while this northern end became an emergency HQ for the Greater London Council – after the storming of County Hall perhaps. The GLC has gone, but trams, or light rail networks as they are now called, are back in Manchester and Sheffield, and maybe soon they will come south to reclaim their tunnel here. Once you have turned right by the tunnel into Fisher Street, the Central School of Art and Design (now the Central and St Martin's School) is on your left, replacing Kingsgate Street where Mrs Gamp, Dickens' grotesque 'midwife and dry nurse' from *Martin Chuzzlewit*, 'lodged at a bird fancier's, next door but one to the celebrated mutton-pie shop, and directly opposite the original cat's meat warehouse'. This was where she and Betsy Prig consumed a tuppenny salad and drank gin from a teapot.

Ahead can be seen the greenery of **RED LION SQUARE**. Go down the right side of its central garden until in front of the four old houses remaining in the Square. Numbers 14 and 15 are, behind their nineteenth-century facades, survivors from the original development of the Square in the 1680s by Nicholas Barbon, a manipulative property speculator easily the match of any around today. He is described in greater detail on page 88. **Number 17** was the unlikely setting for the living-out of a dream of the Middle Ages. Inspired by the leading Pre-Raphaelite poet and painter Dante Gabriel Rossetti, who had earlier occupied the same house

Wrought ironwork above Gray's Inn Walks gates

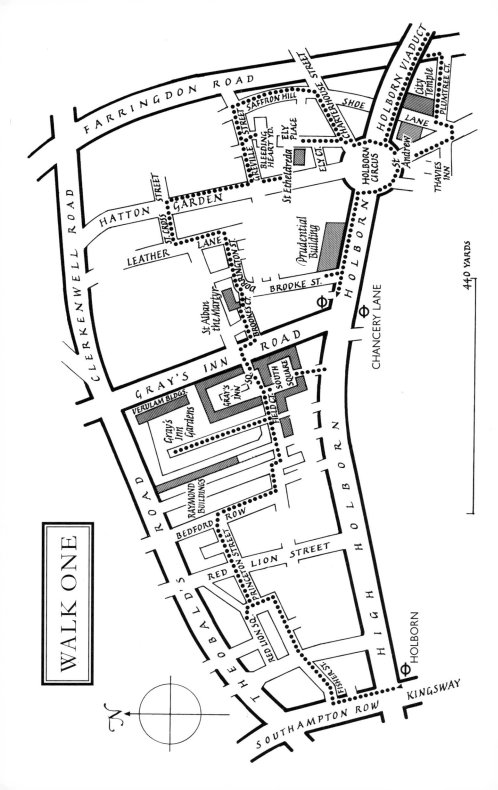

WALK ONE

before moving to the riverside at Blackfriars, two Oxford University friends, William Morris and Edward Burne-Jones, decided, as a second-best to setting up a monastery, to live and work here as medieval handicraftsmen, painting pictures and decorating furniture with scenes from Dante, Malory and Chaucer. It was all a very English version of *la vie bohème*. When not in Oxford helping Rossetti with the murals in the new Union Building (which faded and flaked away as soon as they were completed), they were looked after by 'Red Lion Mary' who, in Burne-Jones' words, could supply 'victuals and squalor at all hours', and read him the newspaper while he painted.

In 1859 marriage intervened and the household broke up, but by 1861 a new enterprise came together at number 8 Red Lion Square (demolished), with the grandiose title of Morris, Marshall, Faulkner & Co. It was to be perhaps the most distinguished interior decoration and church furnishing company yet seen, with Morris designing his furniture, fabrics and wallpapers, and a kiln in the basement for the tiles and stained glass to be designed by him and Burne-Jones. Rossetti and Ford Madox Brown also worked for the firm, and Philip Webb was the architect member. (Webb will appear again in Lincoln's Inn Fields, p. 40.) Morris took the firm north to Queen Square when he went to live there in 1865.

How they would all have loathed the mean pink-brick block of 1960s council flats next to number 17. Pass swiftly by it and dwell instead on the **Conway Hall** (1929) in the north-east corner of the Square, not because it is a thing of great beauty, either, but because it is the home of the South Place Ethical Society, rendez-vous of those who find themselves in agreement with T. H. Huxley, that God is no more than 'a gaseous invertebrate'. There was a Unitarian congregation at South Place, Finsbury which in 1864 acquired as its minister a Virginian of patrician stock called Moncure Conway. By 1869 this body had become agnostic in its leanings; in 1897 it took its present name. Instead of a minister it has 'an Appointed Lecturer' to further 'the study and dissemination of ethical principles, and the cultivation of a rational and humane way of life'. Fenner Brockway – Labour MP, imprisoned for his conscientious objection in World War One and a founder of CND – was one of the most distinguished of recent lecturers. His statue shares the

Left: Fenner Brockway in full flow in Red Lion Square, hoist by his own gesture, his kipper tie already a nice period detail
Right: A Bedford Row fanlight and door frame

Square garden with a bust of the philosopher Bertrand Russell, who was also a 'conchie' and a CND supporter. Once there was an obelisk in the middle of the garden with a Latin inscription on it asking 'What are you looking at, stranger? Go away.'

Russell was one of the Bloomsbury Group, that network of painters and writers including Duncan Grant, Virginia Woolf and Lytton Strachey, identified with the area immediately to the northwest. As you walk eastwards from Red Lion Square along the otherwise undistinguished **Princeton Street**, you will come upon the shop of Cressida Bell, granddaughter of Virginia's sister Vanessa Bell, full of scarves, throws, fabrics and lampshades, some clearly descended from the designs of the Bloomsberries. At the end of Princeton Street the wide expanse of **Bedford Row** opens on either side, one of London's best collections of eighteenth-century town houses, lit by a range of varied fanlights above door hoods on carved brackets, and shaded by false acacia trees. Numbers 36 and 43 are in fact probably late seventeenth-century, built by Nicholas Barbon again, but the rest are about 1720. The fanlight at number 36 is one of London's earliest. If strolling in good-mannered streets like this comes as a particular balm to your soul, turn left and wander northwards through Great James Street, Rugby Street, and Great Ormond Street for ten minutes, though these are strictly outside our area. (I have been snide about the GLC earlier so it is only right to give its Historic Buildings Division credit for its defence of this area in the 1960s, and Camden Council in the 1970s.) Otherwise, turn right and then follow Bedford Row round past the water pump in the middle of the road to one of Gray's Inn's many entrances.

The earliest surviving records of **GRAY'S INN** date from 1569, by which time it had long been a thriving community, and one must take on trust that its name derives from the family who owned the land on which it is built: Sir Reginald Le Grey, Chief Justice of Chester, died in 1308. Its glory days were in the sixteenth century when it was by far the largest Inn, with the most distinguished membership, including Queen Elizabeth's trusted counsellors William Cecil, Francis Walsingham and Nicholas Bacon, and his more distinguished son, Francis. Shakespeare's patron, the Earl of Southampton, Sir Philip Sidney, the paragon of the age, and one Lawrence Washington from Northamptonshire were also of its number. The countryside came right up to its northern edge, so it was easy to escape for recreation and the air was felt to be healthy.

Earlier in the century, in 1526, the Inn performed a masque showing that 'Lord Governance was ruled by Dissipation and Negligence', which caused Vox Populi and other personifications to expel them. It also caused Cardinal Wolsey, Henry VIII's chief minister, to send the masque's author to gaol, because he detected an attack on himself. At the festivities for the Christmas of 1594 a performance, possibly the first, of Shakespeare's *Comedy of Errors* was given in the Hall. There was meant to be a joint party with the men of the Inner Temple, but such was the scrum that it had to be abandoned and the play hastily substituted. On Twelfth Night, the entertainment took the form of 'Envy, Malcontent, and Folly' being brought in, captives, their attempts against the state of 'Graya' having been frustrated. In the same year Francis Bacon's puritan mother had written to his brother, 'I trust that they will not mum, masque nor sinfully revel at Gray's Inn.' In 1613 there were great festivities for the marriage of King James I's daughter Elizabeth to the Elector Palatine, the Protestant ruler of the Rhineland in Germany. Gray's Inn cooperated with the Inner Temple in a masque, contrived by Francis Bacon in spite of his mother. 'They made choice to come by water [to Westminster] which suited well enough their device, which was the marriage of the river of Thames to the Rhine', said the Jacobean letter-writer John Chamberlain. When they arrived the king was too fatigued to receive them. However, he allowed them to return a few days later, and was so pleased by the performance that they were invited back for dinner, paid for by a winning bet James had with the Elector and his followers over 'running at the ring' (tilting at a target).

On Twelfth Night in 1623, the members of Gray's Inn borrowed some small cannon from the Tower of London as part of their masquing. When they were fired the timid King James was reported to have started from his bed, crying, ' Treason, Treason'. By this time Francis Bacon had fallen from favour, after accusations of taking bribes had lost him the Lord Chancellorship: 'Myself for quiet and the better to hold out am retired to Gray's Inn; for when my chief friends were gone so far off, it was time for me to go to a cell.' Two years later he died, a martyr to the new spirit of scientific enquiry, after catching cold when trying to preserve a chicken carcase by stuffing it with snow.

By 1656, in the stern days of Oliver Cromwell's rule, the benchers of the Inn were noting with disapproval the throwing of bread by junior members in Hall. In 1684 members sallied forth to fight a pitched battle with Nicholas Barbon's workmen in a doomed attempt to stop his development of Red Lion Fields. In 1685 a member by the name of Richard Nelthorp was executed before the main gate of the Inn for taking part in the Duke of Monmouth's rebellion against his uncle King James II, and a student called Bird was hung at Tyburn in 1691 for murdering his girl bride.

The eighteenth century was a period of decline and bad finances for Gray's and the other three Inns, partly offset by allowing shops to be set up in their buildings. Thomas Osborne, the publisher and bookseller, was one of them, only really remembered today because Dr Johnson was employed by him as a cata-

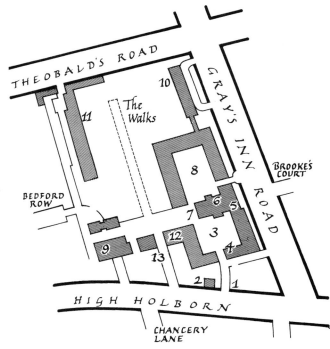

GRAY'S INN

1 Entrance
2 The Cittie of Yorke
3 South Square
4 Dickens' office
5 Library
6 Chapel
7 Hall
8 The Square
9 Council of Legal Education
10 Verulam Buildings
11 Raymond Buildings
12 Field Court
13 Fulwood Place

loguer early in his London career and had to put him in his place: 'Sir, he was impertinent to me, and I beat him.' Johnson told Boswell the claim that this took place in Osborne's shop was wrong, and there is no evidence of him having used a folio volume of the Septuagint (the 1594 edition) to fell him, or that Johnson then put his foot on his neck: a pity. Richard and Jacob Tonson, much more distinguished late seventeenth- and eighteenth-century publishers, had their shop in Gray's Inn gateway, on Gray's Inn Road. They profited greatly from *Paradise Lost*, whose copyright they bought from another publisher, and from Dryden's works. Jacob had moved to the Strand by the time he became publisher of the *Spectator*.

In 1803 the ugly Verulam Buildings were erected, followed by Raymond Buildings in 1825. Women were now allowed to reside, which meant that families could live in the Inn. But the membership was lacking in distinction compared to the other Inns; Gray's was furthest from the new Law Courts in the Strand, which made it unattractive to intending barristers. In 1870 some scholarships were set up to try and attract more new men, but by 1891 there were a mere sixteen benchers and the overdraft was growing unchecked. It was only at the end of that decade that the Inn's affairs were put in order. In this century, Hilaire Belloc, Sidney Webb and F. E. Smith were famous names amongst the members. Smith (Lord Birkenhead) had much to do with the flourishing state of the Inn between the wars.

If you look to the left after entering the Inn from Bedford Row, you can see the long grey range of **Raymond Buildings** with Atkin Building tacked onto the end. Towards the end of 1827, the firm of Ellis and Blackmore, solicitors, took up residence at number 1, bringing with them the young Charles Dickens. He had joined them as a clerk in May, when they were still at number 1 South Square, Gray's Inn (then called Holborn Court). From the upper windows of Raymond Buildings he spat out cherry stones onto the hats of those below and nursed his hatred of the Law's corruptions and delay. 'Imagination gloats over the fullness of time when the staircases shall have quite tumbled down – they are daily wearing into an ill-savoured powder, but have not quite tumbled down yet – when the last prolix old bencher, all of the oldentime, shall have been got out of an upper window by means of a fire ladder . . .' (*Uncommercial Traveller*). On the right of the entrance from Bedford Row is a low building with some delightful Trafalgar balconies, but it was surely a mistake to paint them duck-egg blue.

Go to the right and then immediately left into **Field Court**. Number 2 is of 1780, whereas number 3 is 1935, but both have enviable views up **Gray's Inn Walks** – the garden. At lunchtime one can go through the wrought-iron gates and pace their length – Charles Lamb called them 'altogether reverend and law breathing', though their grave character was encroached on by the anchoring of a barrage balloon there in the last war. The initials on the gates, which appear to be TWIG, are in fact for 'Treasurer, William Gilbey'. Go down the avenue of recently planted oaks of various species, and you will come to the relics of two ancient catalpas, Indian bean trees. That on the left is alleged to be the self-same that Francis Bacon planted when he laid out the gardens in 1606, grown from slips brought back from America by Sir Walter Raleigh. Through the railings at the end of the Walks is Theobalds Road where, at number 22, was born Benjamin Disraeli. St John Street leads northward before becoming Doughty

Gray's Inn gryphons
Lunchtime in Gray's Inn
Walks; Raymond Buildings
behind the plane tree

Street where Dickens lived, between 1837 and 1839, at number 48. This house is outside this book's area, but is now a museum and worth the detour for any devotee.

Returning through the gates, it is worth looking at the two quite witty newish stone gryphons (the Inn's badge) guarding the way to Fulwood Place. Do not go down there, but walk instead through the passage to the left, from which you emerge into **Gray's Inn Square**. About half of this was destroyed in the air raids of May 1941, but has been skilfully recreated. The Chapel, Hall and Library all succumbed to the same raids. In the new **Chapel**, the maple woodwork was the gift of the Canadian Bar Association, whilst the new **Hall** roof, which used up to 160 Kentish oak trees, was the gift of the American Bar Association. Luckily the Hall screen, pictures, escutcheons from the panelling, and stained glass had already been dismantled and so were saved; they are now reinstalled in the new Hall. The new south oriel window is also the gift of the Americans. The **Library** lost 32,000 volumes in the bombing, but 800 of the most valuable had already been moved to

Left:Francis Bacon in South Square, Gray's Inn
Right:Gray's Inn Hall, rebuilt after the Blitz

safety. **South Square**, on the other side of the Hall and Chapel, with a statue of Francis Bacon in the middle, also suffered grievously in the bombing, only number 1, where Dickens clerked for a few months, surviving intact.

Before the nineteenth-century reforms, the Court of the Exchequer used to hold out-of-term sittings in the Hall. In 1901 the arms of that great magnate Charles Brandon, Duke of Suffolk, who married a daughter of Henry VII, were found under some plaster above its north door. One of his descendants was the unfortunate Lady Jane Grey, whose Protestant supporters claimed the throne on her behalf for a few days in 1554, before Catholic Queen Mary ousted her and then deprived her of her head. The benchers must have decided it was impolitic to leave such a visible link to a discredited line. Likewise, in Elizabeth's reign, the Earl of Northumberland's arms had to be removed, after he took part in the Revolt of the Northern Earls against her in 1569. A few years before 1901 a remarkable triangular stove, with a grate on each side, was removed from its position in the centre of the Hall. Before its

*Left: Eduardo Paolozzi's statue of himself as the blacksmith-god Hephaestus, at
34-36 High Holborn, a few yards to the west of the Cittie of Yorke
Right: Warwick Court, leading from Gray's Inn to Chancery Lane*

installation in 1815 the only source of heat had been an open fire,
without a chimney, the smoke from which had to make its own way
up to vents in the roof. This stove is now to be found in a pub, The
Cittie of Yorke, formerly Henekey's Wine Lodge, beside the High
Holborn gateway to the Inn. The passageway out of the south side
of South Square will take you there.

   After a quick one, retrace your steps to the Square and leave the
Inn by its gateway into Gray's Inn Road. Take the zebra crossing
here and recall that moment in the mid-seventeenth century when
John Aubrey, author of *Brief Lives*, 'was in great danger of being
killed by a drunkard in the street opposite Graye's-Inn gate – a
gentleman whom I never sawe before, but (Deo Gratias) one of his
companions hindred his thrust.' Walk a few yards to the right
before turning left into Brooke's Court. Ahead you will see the
idiosyncratic saddleback tower of **ST ALBAN THE MARTYR**,
with a staircase turret running up its middle. The entrance to the
church is through the archway by the attached clergy house and

then across the small courtyard. The original church, of which only the tower survived the 1941 bombing, was built in 1861–2 by William Butterfield, in polychrome brick, stone and terracotta, to bring some High Anglican colour into the encircling slums. It must have been a worthy consort to Butterfield's famous church of All Saints built in Margaret Street, north-east of Oxford Circus, a few years before - the two of them prime examples of Victorian Gothic influenced by the ideas which John Ruskin had gleaned in northern Italy, but also speaking strongly of Butterfield's forceful individuality. Father Mackonochie, its first priest, and his curate Father Stanton both sound to have been saintly men, devoted to their parishioners, many of whom lived in a state of savagery. But they were much vexed by various prosecutions on charges of ritualism. The low-church Lord Shaftesbury, who himself did so much to improve the lot of the poor, visited St Alban's in 1866 and reported that 'in outward form and ritual it is the worship of Jupiter or Juno'.

What we see inside the church now is a nave by Adrian Gilbert Scott (1961), brother of Giles, the architect of Liverpool Anglican Cathedral, and grandson of Sir George Gilbert Scott, architect of St Pancras Station and the Albert Memorial. With its internal buttresses threaded by passage-like aisles, it echoes another of London's great Victorian churches, J. L. Pearson's St Augustine's in Kilburn, which in turn derives from the medieval cathedral of Albi in southern France. It is a noble space, pretty much ruined by a mural (1966) at the east end and stations of the cross (1970) on the side walls, both by Hans Feibusch, employing a gruesome palette.

On leaving, Butterfield's **clergy house** is worth a closer look, for here can be seen the trick which he played in a number of his vicarages and houses – combining Gothic arches with sash windows, a harbinger of the softer, more feminine 'Queen Anne' style soon to emerge. Once through the archway, turn left along what is Dorrington Street, although there is no sign to tell you so. This will bring you into **Leather Lane** with its street market stalls selling a ripe mixture of clothes, handbags, CDs, and fruit-and-veg. A stroll to the left and then a turn to the right into St Cross Street will bring you, at the junction with Hatton Garden, to the **Parochial School** of Saint Andrew's Church, Holborn. It was built by Sir Christopher Wren's master mason, Mark Strong, and although gutted in

*Hatton Garden: a sculpture on the
Treasure House and diamond dealers'
shop signs*

the Blitz and now converted into business premises, it still has the
painted figures of a charity girl and boy outside.

Return south down **Hatton Garden**, home to London's diamond merchants and jewellery trade, passing one of Johnson
Matthey's buildings on the way. This firm of bullion dealers nearly
came to grief a few years ago and had to be rescued by the Bank of
England. It is worth walking down as far as numbers 19–21, the
aptly named Treasure House, for the sake of the vigorous bas
reliefs – blacksmith, miner, silversmith, two female nudes –
adorning it, before returning to the junction with Greville Street.
Turn right into it and soon the entrance to **Bleeding Heart Yard**
will be seen on the right. There are a number of explanations of
the name, including one linking it to Lady Elizabeth Hatton. The
neighbourhood had been granted by Queen Elizabeth to one of
her favourites, Sir Christopher Hatton, a Lord Chancellor with
whom she delighted to dance. Lady Elizabeth is said to have been
killed by one of her admirers, in 1648. When her corpse was found

Left: Bleeding Heart Yard Right: A Victorian-Gothic warehouse by Saffron Hill

next morning, her heart was still pumping blood. The other theories about the yard's name will be found set out by Dickens in *Little Dorrit*, where he called it 'a place much changed in feature and fortune, yet with some relish of ancient greatness about it'. He made it the home of Mr Plornish the plasterer, 'long in the legs, yielding at the knees, foolish in the face, flannel-jacketed, lime-whitened . . . one of those many wayfarers on the road of life, who seem to be afflicted with supernatural corns, rendering it impossible for them to keep up even with their lame competitors.'

Dickens' 'relish' has finally forsaken it now so, after a quick look, turn right out of it and go down the slope, pausing before turning right into **Saffron Hill** for a good look at the splendiferous Victorian Gothic warehouse on the corner, actually number 25 Farringdon Road. It speaks of vigorous commercial pride, each of its yellow-brick pilasters topped by a differently carved stone capital, the stone tracery of the window tops supported by cast-iron columns, the whole finished off with a jaunty pepperpot turret. Saffron Hill was where Dickens located the Three Cripples pub in *Oliver Twist*, patronised by Bill Sikes, Nancy and Fagin. Fagin lived

Ely Place, a dignified eighteenth-century development spoilt by the twentieth century

in Field Lane nearby (swept away when Holborn Viaduct was built in 1869): 'In its filthy shops are exposed for sale huge bunches of second-hand silk handkerchiefs ... for here reside the traders who purchase them from pick-pockets' – like the Artful Dodger.

Go up the steps at the south end of Saffron Hill and turn right until you come to the entrance to **ELY PLACE**. Here was the palace of the medieval Bishops of Ely: 'My lord of Ely, when I was last in Holborn I saw good strawberries in your garden there ...' said Shakespeare's Richard III. But in Elizabeth's reign Bishop Cox was unwise enough to remonstrate with the Queen over her order against resident women in cathedral closes. He compounded his error by marrying a young widow when he was seventy. Elizabeth exacted her revenge by forcing him to lease the manor to her so she in turn could bestow it on her favourite, Sir Christopher Hatton. All that is left of the palace is its chapel, now the Roman Catholic church of **St Etheldreda**; she was abbess of Ely in the seventh century. It has the distinction of being the only example of work from the reign of King Edward I (c. 1290) to survive in London, apart from Westminster Abbey. For those alive to such nuances, it is on the cusp between Geometrical and early Decorated, and is embellished, if that is the right word, with much post-war stained glass and polystyrene statuary of English martyrs. In effect, it is a double-decker church, because it has a sizeable undercroft which is also used.

Ely Place was developed in the 1770s and a good number of the sober Georgian houses erected then survive. St Etheldreda's served as a church for the new inhabitants until 1833 when it was leased to a Welsh congregation, before the Roman Catholics were eventually able to buy it in 1874. There is the chance for refreshment down the alley called Ely Court, just to the south of the church, where **The Mitre** pub will be found. It was established in 1546, for the bishops' servants, and until quite recently its bars used to shut at different times, one keeping London licensing hours and the other those imposed by the licensing magistrates of the Isle of Ely, a legal quirk perhaps in some way connected with the status of Ely Place as a species of sanctuary from the law. In theory the police could not enter, except by invitation. The Mitre has the trunk of a cherry tree around which, it is confidently asserted, Queen Elizabeth danced. If the gate at the north end of Ely Place were ever open, you would be able to enter Bleeding Heart Yard (p. 23) from this direction.

Coming out of Ely Place, cross straight over Charterhouse Street and Holborn, southwards to **ST ANDREW, HOLBORN**. As you do so you will pass a building occupying the apex formed by these two streets, which is the London headquarters of De Beers' central selling organisation. It is the most important rough diamond distribution centre, handling 80 per cent of the world output. St Andrew is the largest of Wren's parish churches, built between 1684 and 1690, though it does incorporate some mid fifteenth-century work, as will be clear when you look at the chapel at the bottom of the tower. On the subject of size, Wren said, ' The Romanists may build larger churches, it is enough if they hear the murmur of mass, but ours are to be fitted for auditories.' In other words, for Protestants what mattered was being able to hear the word of God, and the sermon based on it. The church was gutted during the Blitz and only reopened in 1960.

In 1808 William Hazlitt the critic was married here, with

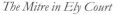
The Mitre in Ely Court

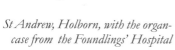
St Andrew, Holborn, with the organ-case from the Foundlings' Hospital

Charles Lamb, that delightful character and now rather unfashionable author, as his best man. Charles's intermittently mad sister Mary, who had killed their mother and with whom he wrote the *Tales From Shakespeare*, was a bridesmaid. In 1815 in a letter to Robert Southey, by then Poet Laureate, Lamb reminisced: 'I was at Hazlitt's marriage and had like to have been turned out several times during the ceremony. Anything awful makes me laugh. I misbehaved once at a funeral.' Hazlitt was also to reminisce, on his first meeting with Lamb. He was disputing with, among others, Coleridge and Godwin, 'which was the best, Man as he was, or as he is to be. "Give me", says Lamb, "Man as he is *not* to be." ' In 1817 the twelve-year-old Benjamin Disraeli was baptised here, after his father Isaac fell out with the elders of the Bevis Marks synagogue. In 1827 a young surgeon called William Marsden found a woman dying on the churchyard steps and could not get her admitted to a hospital, so the following year he founded the Royal Free Hospital in Gray's Inn Road, since removed to Hampstead. You will see a blue plaque to him on number 65, Lincoln's Inn Fields.

In 1961 the monument to Captain Thomas Coram was installed in the church. He established the Foundlings' Hospital, for the sustenance of abandoned children, in the north of the parish in 1742. When that was demolished in 1926, various fixtures from its chapel were saved and now grace St Andrew: the captain's monument, the font, the pulpit, the organ case. Since 1991 the church has been the headquarters of the Royal College of Organists. The interior is all in apple-pie order, full of fresh paint, polished wood, gilt, and daylight; a peculiar (? late seventeenth-century) carving of the Last Judgement is fixed to the exterior on the left of the entry door, while two painted charity children, like those on the Parochial School (p. 22), look westward from the tower.

Behind St Andrew, on the **HOLBORN VIADUCT**, is the **City Temple** of the United Reformed Church (1874), its tower very much in the Wren mode and making a good juxtaposition with St Andrew's. The Viaduct was built (1869) to speed the traffic to and from the centre of the City. Horses would no longer have to brake going down into or strain pulling up out of the bed of the old Fleet river, which had been covered over in the mid-eighteenth century. It was seized on by the City fathers for an unbridled display of corporation heraldry; everywhere you look, whether on top, on the sides, or underneath, the winged helmet crest and the dragon supporters – or indeed the whole coat of arms – is repeated. (The dragon often gets called a gryphon or griffin, but that is inaccurate. A gryphon, as sported by Gray's Inn, is concocted from the head of an eagle and the body of a lion; there is nothing aquiline or leonine about the scaly, winged monster of the City.) As if all these symbols were not enough, the parapets of the bridge also groan under the weight of four winged lions each with a ball trapped neatly under its left paw, various lamp standards, and four well-built bronze ladies, exuding Victorian earnestness in their personifications of Commerce, Science, Agriculture and Fine Art. How much of the last we have here must be in doubt, but it is all enormous fun. So too are the twin buildings at either end of the viaduct. **Fitz Eylwin House** at the western end is named after the first Lord Mayor of London, while **Gresham House** at the east end honours Sir Thomas, founder of Gresham College and the Royal Exchange, who lent his name to Gresham's Law: bad money driving out good. Statues of each can be seen on the buildings' frontages. (There were once two matching buildings on the north side – named after Sir Hugh Myddleton, the Elizabethan entrepreneur behind the New River water supply scheme for London, and Sir William Walworth, the Lord Mayor and Fishmonger who slew Wat Tyler, leader of the Peasants' Revolt in 1381, in the presence of the young King Richard II.) They are ornate but elegant essays in Portland stone and Victorian Gothic and, like the bridge, are well peppered with winged dragons. Each incorporates a very generous public staircase, to take one down to Farringdon Street below, lit from above by an open colonnade at what, from the viaduct's point of view, is ground level. Do not omit to go downstairs, for only from there can the red-and-gilt cast ironwork of the viaduct be really appreciated (it can be felt trembling like a thoroughbred when a double-decker bus goes over it). The atlantes supporting the second-floor balconies are also best seen from below. Look too at the bearded heads on the keystones of the arches down here, one with grapes, one with hops, and one, poor fellow, with *fish* entwined in his hair.

Left: Holborn Viaduct with Gresham House behind
Right: Prince Albert rises above it all at Holborn Circus. The Prudential Building is on the right

Assuming you have taken my advice and are in Farringdon Street, go a few yards down it and turn right up Plumtree Court. Unless you are a satisfied customer of Coopers and Lybrand the accountants (on the left), the best thing about it is its name. At the top swing left and then right so that you find yourself walking past **St Andrew's rectory and courthouse**, built by S. S. Teulon in 1871. He was one of the 'rogue Goths', prepared to commit all sorts of violations in the name of the style so long as the result had 'go'. To your left is the site, but the site only, of **Thavies Inn**, one of the Inns of Chancery (see p. 116). When there was still something of the buildings to be seen in Dickens' day, he described it in *Bleak House* as 'a narrow street of high houses, like an oblong cistern to hold the fog'. (The armourer John Thavies' endowment of St Andrew in 1348 still helps to maintain it.) Ahead is **Holborn Circus** with Prince Albert on his horse, waving his hat, in the middle. 'Peace' sits at one end of the horse and 'History' at the other, sisters perhaps of the personifications on Holborn Viaduct. They dispute possession of the island with various traffic lights and lamp standards stuck there with total insensitivity. David Piper, in his incomparable *Companion Guide to London*, may have said it has 'strong claims to be the most idiotic statue in London', but there was no need to add to the mockery with all this assorted 'street furniture'.

Westward up **Holborn** now, along the north pavement, averting your eye from the dead slab of the old *Daily Mirror* building (1960) to your left, which shouldn't be there much longer since there are plans afoot for three buildings by Norman Foster on its site, and from the brassy-windowed horror that has replaced the old Gamages store on your right. After these examples of the architectural efforts of the last forty years, who can afford to be snooty about Alfred Waterhouse's **Prudential Assurance Building** (1879, 1899–1906) any longer? Its stock may not have risen in the same way as his Natural History Museum in South Kensington or his Manchester Town Hall, and it is hard to swallow the aggressive salmon-pink and carbolic-red 'Slaughterhouse' colours of the brickwork and terracotta, as if someone has been heavy-handed with the cochineal, but his eclectic, secular Gothic has vigour and 'assurance', to borrow a word from his client, 'Britain's largest investor'. Certainly his client was happy because this became the 'house style' and colour for Prudential branches round the country. Waterhouse did twenty-seven building projects for them. Go under the entry arch and feast on the quality of the rib vaulting above you, before passing on, under the bridge of sighs, to look at the cloister effect achieved in the courtyard beyond, 'Waterhouse Square'. Look down through the new glass dome in the centre of the courtyard for a glimpse of an alarming day-glo mobile hanging below and then go over to the memorial to 'Prudential Men' who died in the First World War, by F. V. Blundstone. A slumped, seated soldier, bare-headed, open-necked, is about to be crowned with a wreath by two winged and bare-breasted girls. At each corner stands another bare-breasted girl, a wreath in one hand and either a ship, a plane, a shell or a field-gun tucked under the other arm. At the start of 1995 the 'Man from the Pru', calling from door to door to collect insurance payments, finally disappeared from the streets, killed off by direct debit. Perhaps a small memorial to this enduring source of human contact and advice could join the others in this courtyard.

As you head for the gateway again, look through the windows of

The Prudential Building: the war memorial and the bridge of sighs

the main hall which occupies the Holborn frontage on the left. It is lined with cream, mustard and brown glazed faience tile and brick. The Pru Building occupies the site of another Inn of Chancery, Furnival's, finally dissolved in 1818. In the 1830s, Dickens lived here and began *Pickwick Papers*, before moving to Doughty Street.

Brooke Street runs along the west side of the Pru Building and it was here, in a house on the site of what is now number 39, that the poet **Thomas Chatterton** poisoned himself with arsenic, aged 17, in 1770. He had come up to London from his native Bristol, but unfortunately his patron, the immensely rich Alderman Beckford (father of William Beckford of Fonthill), died almost immediately and funds ran out. Wordsworth called Chatterton, a precursor of the Romantics, 'the marvellous Boy/the Sleepless Soul that perished in his pride', and Keats dedicated *Endymion* to his memory. But the literary reverberations do not stop there. In 1856 an artist called Richard Wallis painted 'The Death of Chatterton', the one picture by which Wallis is remembered. The novelist George Meredith posed for the picture as the dead Chatterton in the very room where he poisoned himself, the dome of St Paul's visible through the open attic window. The next year Meredith's wife, a daughter of the novelist Thomas Love Peacock, left him for Wallis. This in due course inspired Meredith to write *Modern Love*, his sequence of fifty sonnets on the theme of the unfaithful wife:

> But she is mine! Ah, no! I know too well
> I claim a star whose light is overcast:
> I claim a phantom-woman in the Past.
> The hour has struck, though I heard not the bell!
>
> These two were rapid falcons in a snare,
> Condemned to do the flitting of the bat . . .
> Then each applied to each that fatal knife,
> Deep questioning, which probes to endless dole.
> Ah, what a dusty answer gets the soul
> When hot for certainties in this our life!

In the middle of Holborn, almost exactly by Holborn Bars – the silvered dragons marking the City boundary – is the **Royal Fusiliers' War Memorial**, a lone tin-hatted Tommy, his right foot upon a rock, his left arm held out to balance himself, with its fist clenched. He is wary, on watch, holding his rifle with its long (now slightly bent) bayonet at the trail. This regiment, the City of London's own, raised 52 battalions in the First War, according to the list on the statue's plinth, including one for stockbrokers, four for public school recruits, two for sportsmen, one for bankers and one for Jews. Whatever their background, 22,000 of them were killed.

The south side of Holborn is covered on pages 60 to 63, at the end of the Lincoln's Inn Walk. This walk ends here, at Chancery Lane tube. Be warned – it is closed on Sundays, but it is only five minutes' walk onwards along High Holborn to Holborn tube.

The Royal Fusilier guarding the City boundary. On the right, that comparative rarity, a classical building from the 1950s, with the Mirror building, from the same decade, behind

WALK TWO

Lincoln's Inn, the Law Courts, and Chancery Lane

Outside Holborn tube, either turn right and walk eastwards along High Holborn, or turn left and walk southwards down Kingsway. If you take the former option you will be confronted very shortly by the might and splendour of what was the **Pearl Assurance Building.** The grand gates of this piece of Edwardian Baroque (1912), flanked by clusters of Venetian lanterns, are padlocked now, for the Pearl has been taken over and undergone the Peterborough Effect. Let's hope the building finds a new owner up to its grandiosity, then the gates can be unlocked to allow Sir George Frampton's statue of St George in the courtyard to be compared to that other war memorial at the Pru, at the far end of Holborn. The speckled granite of the ground and first floor strikes a bit cold, whilst the dome and columniated drum that crown the building seem attenuated, but such public-spirited attempts to enliven the skyline should always be applauded. Turn right by the expensive public lavatory disguised as a circular Parisian advertising kiosk and go down the alley called **Little Turnstile**. When Lincoln's Inn Fields were just that, this device, and Great Turnstile at the northeast corner, kept the animals from straying. Passing the **Ship Tavern**, where the loos come free with a drink and in whose Elizabethan predecessor Roman Catholic masses were illegally offered up, you will emerge into Lincoln's Inn Fields.

If you take the Kingsway option you will shortly pass the facade of the Roman Catholic church of **St Anselm and St Cecilia**. It is an excellent 1900s essay in eighteenth-century Flemish style and the quality of the creamy stonework inside fulfils any expectations the facade raises. There is a rood loft with rood in situ and a painted organ behind. The proportions of the stone

A cast of the Apollo Belvedere, funerary urns and Chantrey's bust of Sir John Soane, under the dome in his Museum

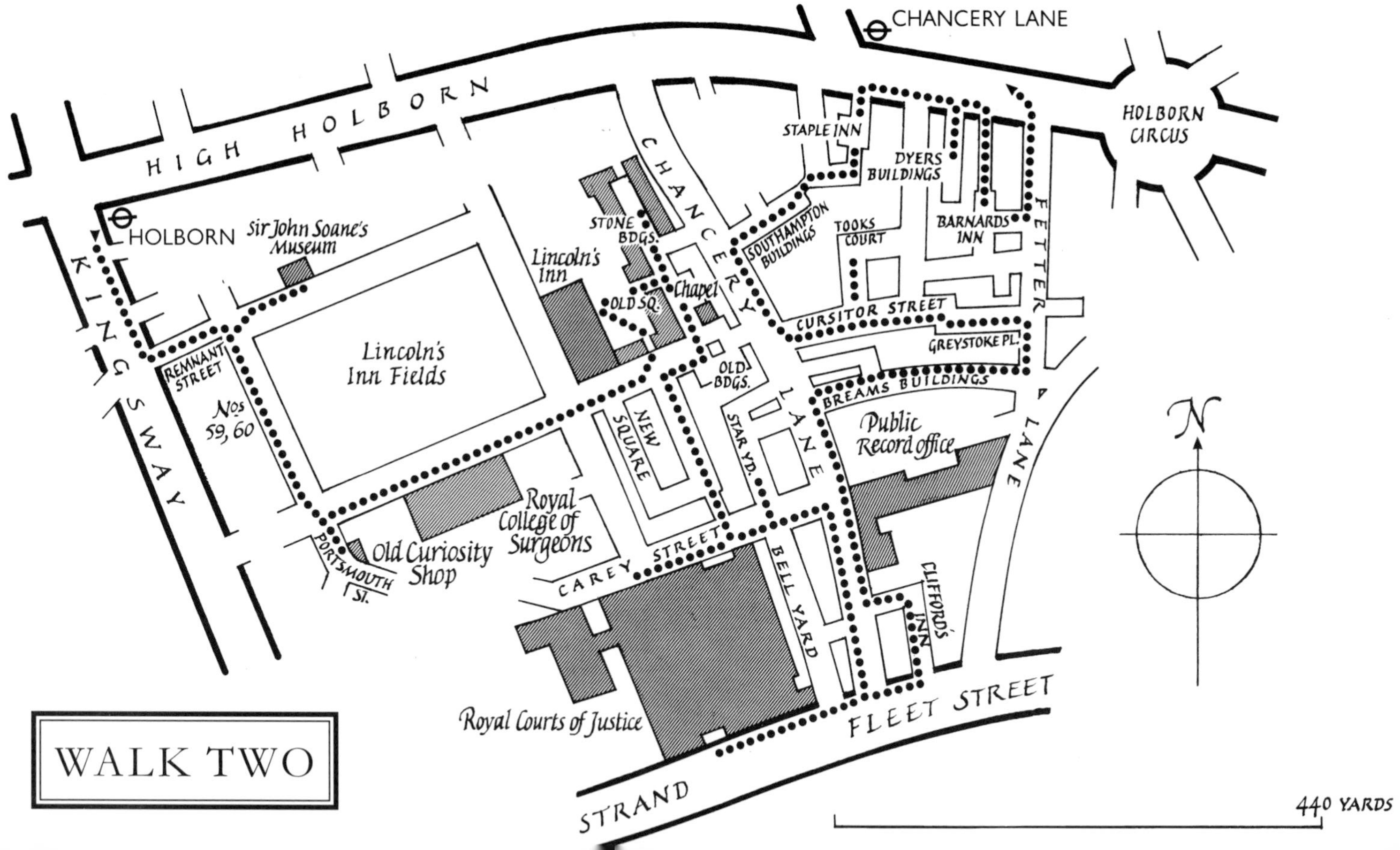

440 YARDS

N

HOLBORN CIRCUS

CHANCERY LANE

FETTER LANE

FLEET STREET

BARNARDS INN

DYERS BUILDINGS

TOOKS COURT

STAPLE INN

SOUTHAMPTON BUILDINGS

CURSITOR STREET

GREYSTOKE PL.

BREAMS BUILDINGS

Public Record office

CLIFFORD'S INN

CHANCERY LANE

STONE BDGS.

OLD SQ.

Chapel

OLD BDGS.

STAR YD.

BELL YARD

Lincoln's Inn

NEW SQUARE

CAREY STREET

Royal Courts of Justice

STRAND

Royal College of Surgeons

Old Curiosity Shop

Lincoln's Inn Fields

Sir John Soane's Museum

HIGH HOLBORN

HOLBORN

PORTSMOUTH STR.

REMNANT STREET

Nos 59, 60

KINGSWAY

WALK TWO

reredos are out of kilter now that the altar has been moved forward to fall in with current fashion. On its right is a Rubensesque painting of the *Deposition* and in the south aisle the Royal Sardinian coat of arms with ebullient carved wooden lion supporters. They are survivors from the eighteenth-century Sardinian Embassy chapel at the south-west corner of Lincoln's Inn Fields. It was then one of the few chapels where mass legally could be heard in London (another was in Moorfields) and received the attentions of the Gordon rioters in 1780 who burnt many of its fittings. It is worth going a little further down Kingsway to look at **number 42** because this was one of Sir Edwin Lutyens' first London commissions and first office buildings (1906), designed shortly after he underwent conversion from Surrey vernacular to Italian High Renaissance style. As he put it in 1903, ' Palladio is the game !!', though in fact it is Sanmicheli whose influence can be seen in the rustication and the Doric columns. The vaulted hall inside appears to have been successfully ruined by the insertion of an extra floor. His client was William Robinson, who wanted new offices for his magazine the *Garden*. He was the great champion of the naturalistic in garden design, so it is ironic that Lutyens was a leader of the move to a more formalistic approach: 'a garden scheme should have a backbone. . .' The buildings on either side of number 42 are pleasing, too.

Retrace your steps a few yards until you come to the stone sculpture of a crouching Roman centurion above a door on the corner of Remnant Street. Turn in left here and after a few more steps **LINCOLN'S INN FIELDS** will open out before you. This was still an open pasture in the sixteenth century, suitable for the hanging, drawing and quartering of the fourteen Babington Plotters in 1586. Their scheme to murder Queen Elizabeth and place Mary Queen of Scots on the throne not only ensured their grisly deaths, but also Mary's in 1587. In 1588, Armada Year, two Roman Catholics, Robert Morton and Hugh More, were also executed here. We will go anti-clockwise round the square.

Early in the seventeenth century, the benchers of Lincoln's Inn had to apply to the Privy Council to get a stop put to building all over the Fields. But development began on the edges in the 1630s with a scheme by one William Newton for thirty-two houses.

Most were built by 1641, including **numbers 59 and 60**, Lindsey House, so called after its first owner, Robert Bertie, the first Earl of Lindsey. He did not enjoy his new London house for long because he became King Charles I's commander-in-chief and was killed at Edgehill, the first battle of the Civil War, in 1642. On the west side of the square, this is the only original building left here and is in a pilastered style that had become part of the stock-in-trade of the London builder by the 1630s. It is loosely associated with the name of Inigo Jones, who introduced the architectural ideas of Palladio to England. **Numbers 57 and 58** are a hundred years younger; by this time the Palladian style had become the new orthodoxy. However, their porch is by Sir John Soane (see p. 41). Dickens' friend and biographer John Forster lived at number 58 and the lawyer in *Bleak House*, Mr Tulkinghorn, has his chambers there: 'in those shrunken fragments of greatness lawyers lie like maggots in nuts'. **Number 66**, the first house you will have passed at the northern end of the west side, is occupied by Farrers, the Queen's solicitors. Lutyens rebuilt it in 1930 in a 'paraphrase' (as Pevsner neatly puts it) of the original 1686 Powis (or Newcastle) House on this site.

Portsmouth Street goes out of the south-west corner and the **Old Curiosity Shop** will be found there, where it has been since about 1567. It can claim to be the oldest retail shop in England, but not that it is the original of Dickens' shop, the most likely location for which was in Orange Street behind the National Gallery. Its simulated-tile fibreglass (or whatever) roof smacks of Disney. The south-west side of the square is occupied by the **Royal College of Surgeons**, easily identifiable by the giant Ionic-columned portico, all that Sir Charles Barry kept of George Dance's previous work in his rebuilding of 1835. The south-east side has the **Land Registry Office** (1906), a rather leaden piece of Jacobethan, shown up by Philip Hardwick's excellent Tudor pastiche New Hall and Library for Lincoln's Inn across the road.

The 'Fields' themselves, in the care of Camden Council, have a hangdog, unloved air to them. Cannot the members of Lincoln's Inn come to their rescue again? For years they were taken over by dossers, but these have been moved on and the only relic of those days is the party of strong-lager drinkers that gathers round the

The Ship Tavern at the south end of Little Turnstile, and Lindsey House, the sole surviving seventeenth-century building in Lincoln's Inn Fields

memorial to Prime Minister Ramsay Macdonald's wife on a sunny afternoon. There are unattractive railings round the various squares of grass, while the shelter in the middle sits in a sea of depressing tarmac and its leaking gutters are full of grass.

This shelter is said to mark the spot where Lord William Russell, the great Whig martyr, was executed in 1683. He opposed the idea of the Catholic James, Duke of York, succeeding his brother Charles II, and was implicated in the Rye House Plot, supposedly to assassinate the two of them on their way back from the races at Newmarket. His devoted wife, heiress of the last Earl of Southampton, brought to his family, the Earls (later Dukes) of Bedford, a dowry in the form of the whole of Bloomsbury. When she came to see her husband on the night before his execution, 'she kept her sorrow so within herself that she gave him no disturbance by their parting. After she was gone he said, "Now the bitterness of death is past" ' (Gilbert Burnet).

Number 26, on the north side, has a very crisp eighteenth-century carving above its front door: what looks like the head of some sort of savage with a crown of curling feathers and a flower necklace. **Number 19** is by Philip Webb, he who was architect to William Morris's firm (see p. 13). There is a faint Tudor feel to the octagonal piers going up the front of these offices (1868–70), but equally there are ingredients, like the rectangular sash windows with glazing bars (borrowed to a degree from Butterfield, p. 22), of the 'Queen Anne' and Arts and Crafts styles that were soon to emerge so strongly and see off Victorian Gothic. But the earnest muscularity of the latter was still putting up a fight against the new, feminine, 'sweetness and light' aesthetic, as shown by Water-house's **numbers 17–18** slap next door, erected in 1871–2. Waterhouse was polite enough to echo Webb's door-hood, which owes little to any previous style, but for the rest he stuck to Gothic. The ground floor's central capital on its twisted column is a nice confection of ferns, and the top of the building sports gargoyles who look as though they have flown in from Notre Dame. There are some satisfying roundels in the railings fronting the building.

Lincoln's Inn Fields, north side: Sir John Soane's Museum and Alfred Waterhouse's Gothic office building

Number 13, **SIR JOHN SOANE'S MUSEUM,** is among the most evocative and enjoyable buildings in London. Open from 10 to 5, Tuesday to Saturday, not only is it free but its staff are friendly too. Soane (1753–1837) was one of Britain's most distinguished architects, and his stock continues to rise as he is fought over by the classicists, modernists and post-modernists. He was a self-made scholarship boy able to benefit from the education and patronage available from the newly founded Royal Academy. He won the Academy's travelling studentship, which allowed him to make his own Grand Tour of Italy, just as other distinguished architects, such as Gibbs, Kent and Robert Adam, had earlier in the century. This stirred a passion in him for the remains of classical architecture and sculpture which went far beyond his requirements as a professional architect, even in an age when the arts of Greece and Rome reigned supreme. It is the fruits of this passion which form the core of his collection at numbers 13, 12 and 14, for all three houses were his and his displays spread out into the back premises and basements of the latter two.

However, the museum is no purist exercise in classical taste. There are ancient Egyptian, Medieval, Renaissance and later objects, as well as distinguished paintings and drawings by Turner, Hogarth, Watteau, Canaletto and others. But still less is it to be visited only for its exhibits. The museum's greatest charm lies in its potent evocation of its creator. He obviously had a strain of the magpie in him, shown not merely in the range of objects he accumulated, but also in the pleasure he took in displaying them with the aid of shiny mirrors, unexpected sources of light, overhead lanterns and coloured glass. He also relished the challenge of squeezing as much as possible into the confines of three terrace houses, employing gadgetry and playing all manner of spatial tricks in the process. Soane was a showman long before the advent of today's curator-showmen, and there are strong echoes of the fairground in his museum.

The magpie element is evident even on the outside of number 13 for, while caryatides copied from those on the Acropolis in Athens look down from second-floor level, below them stick out four pedestals which Soane rescued when working on the medieval Westminster Hall. The first rooms seen inside number

13 are the **Dining-Room** and **Library**. The decorative scheme
here seems to be indebted to the colour plates of interiors discov-
ered at a Roman house in the grounds of the Villa Negroni in
Rome not long before Soane was out there. What Pompeii and
Herculaneum had been to Robert Adam in the 1750s, so the Villa
Negroni finds (the plates of which are hanging in the Breakfast
Parlour) were to Soane. Throughout the scheme he brings mirrors
into play, and indeed the sliding shutters for the windows looking
onto the square are lined with mirrors. The next two rooms, the
Little Study and the **Dressing-Room**, not much more than sub-
divisions within a passage, illustrate Soane's delight in the frugal
and ingenious use of space. Note the table that emerges from the
knee-hole of the desk in the study, and the walls encrusted with
antique marble fragments. Quite apart from their decorative func-
tion, Soane no doubt also used them and the countless other orig-
inals and casts in the house as visual references for himself and his
pupils, and as the equivalent of the modern decorator's fabric
samples to show to his clients. In the Dressing Room there is the
drawing of the 'Canine Residence' or 'A Dog House designed for a
Nobleman', which Soane did to flatter the 'Mitred Earl', Frederick
Augustus Hervey, 4th Earl of Bristol and Bishop of Derry. He
travelled in Hervey's train round Italy, but the hoped-for commissions at Downhill in Ireland or Ickworth in Suffolk were never to
materialise from that vacillating prelate.

So one moves on, baffled at first by how the **Colonnade** can be
lit in spite of the **Students' Room** above it, and so amazed by the
ingenuity of the triple, hinged, hanging arrangements in the
Picture Room that it is very hard to force oneself actually to look
at the pictures displayed there. But one must, for besides Piranesi's
drawings of the Greek temples at Paestum, the classical ruins by
Clérisseau and Gandy's coloured architectural drawings of designs
by Soane, there are two of Hogarth's great sequences (six paintings in each) – 'A Rake's Progress' and 'An Election'. The joy of
these lies in their detail and clutter, much as the pleasure of the
Museum does. Perhaps this is why Soane bought them.

Downstairs is Soane's elaborate joke, the **Monk's Parlour** and
Yard, decked out with all sorts of gothick bric-à-brac as well as the
skeleton from his friend the sculptor Flaxman's studio. Then

comes the Egyptian **Sarcophagus of Seti I,** helpfully covered with hieroglyphic texts from what was in effect a handbook to the underworld, and lit via an open well by the **Dome** two stories above it.

Upstairs again, one threads a path through the columns, between the herds of gryphons and the funerary urns, and behind a cast of the Apollo Belvedere, while metaphorically ducking the eggs and darts and pushing back the acanthus leaves, until the **Breakfast Parlour** is reached. This is archetypal Soane, with, in his words, its 'spherical ceiling, springing from four segmental arches . . . the spandrels of the dome and the soffits of the arches decorated with a number of mirrors [the whole presenting] a succession of those fanciful effects which constitute the poetry of Architecture'. It is very seldom that from one room or space you cannot get a foretaste view of another – above, below or to one side – and that is certainly true here. It only remains to climb the stairs to the first floor, paying one's respects at the Shakespeare shrine on the way, to be dazzled by the **Drawing Rooms**, recently done out in Soane's authentic 'patent-yellow'.

Soane, with justification, hated his surviving son, so secured an Act of Parliament to preserve his home and collection for the public after his death. Would that he could have done the same for his works. His masterpiece, the Bank of England, has largely gone, as have the law courts at Westminster. You have to go to Pitshanger Manor in Ealing (his own country retreat), or Dulwich Picture Gallery, to see his secular work in London, though every surviving red telephone kiosk owes a debt to him. When designing the kiosk, Giles Gilbert Scott drew on Soane's family monument, which is in old St Pancras churchyard, and on a detail of the mausoleum at Dulwich.

Return now to the south-east corner of the Fields and enter **LINCOLN'S INN** by the pseudo-Tudor gateway, which manages to look like a cruet set, yet get away with it. The origins of the name have been the subject of deep research, the latest view being that the Inn began life on land owned by Henry de Lacy, Earl of Lincoln. It apparently only moved to its present site early in the fifteenth century, before that occupying what became Thavies Inn (p. 30) and then Furnival's Inn (p. 32). After this peripatetic start, it

Lincoln's Inn: The cruet-set gateway with the New Hall by Philip Hardwick behind; and Sir George Gilbert Scott's eastwards extension of Hardwick's Library

then erected the first big building for lawyers in London: the Old Hall of 1490–2, which still stands. The Gatehouse (1518) on Chancery Lane and Old Buildings followed. The Gatehouse bears the arms of Henry VIII, the Earl of Lincoln, and Sir Thomas Lovell, who fought at the Battle of Bosworth in 1485 (which won the throne for the Tudors), and then was Chancellor of the Exchequer to both Henry VII and Henry VIII. He gave a third of the cost of the Gatehouse to the Inn, while the rest of the money had to be borrowed from Sir John Spencer, ancestor of the present Princess of Wales. Another source of income thought up in the sixteenth century was a fine of £5 on any member of the Inn found fornicating in his chamber. If, however, the offence were committed in Chancery Lane, in the Inn garden or rabbit warren, then the fine was £1. In spite of this ploy, it was only in 1580 that the Inn was able to buy the freehold of its site from the Bishop of Chichester.

John Aubrey relates how in the 1580s young Ben Jonson, the future playwright, was helping his stepfather, a bricklayer, to build the 'garden wall of Lincoln's Inn next to Chancery Lane and that a knight, a bencher, walking thro', and hearing him repeat some Greeke verses out of Homer, discoursing with him and finding him to have a witt extraordinary, gave hime some exhibition to maintaine him at Trinity College in Cambridge.'

In November 1602, 'one Vennar of Lincoln's Inn gave out bills of a famous play . . . on the Bankside, to be acted only by certain gentlemen and gentlewomen of account. The price at coming in was two shillings . . . and when he had gotten most part of the money into his hands, he would have shown them a fair pair of heels.' However, he was caught, and the common people 'revenged themselves' on the furnishings of the Swan Theatre. In 1613, the Inn joined with the Middle Temple to present a masque in honour of the Princess Elizabeth's marriage, just like Gray's Inn (p. 16). As well as the twelve masquers, there were 'a dozen little boys dressed like baboons that served for an antimasque' (Chamberlain). However, as the seventeenth century progressed the Inn, with its new Chapel completed in 1623, increasingly became a hotbed of puritanism, producing among others the fanatical William Prynne, author of an attack on stage plays entitled *Histrio-Mastix* which was construed as a slight on Charles I's queen, Henrietta Maria. He was prosecuted by the Attorney-General, William Noy, also of Lincoln's Inn, and was fined, imprisoned and had his ears clipped. Noy, according to Aubrey, was 'a great Humorist . . . He caused the breeches of a bencher of Lincoln's Inn to be taken-in by a taylor and made him believe he had the dropsie.'

Perhaps the greatest member of the Inn in its early days was Sir Thomas More, though to find a statue of him you must go out into Carey Street. In the late eighteenth and early nineteenth centuries it produced some colourful characters like Lords Chancellor Lyndhurst and Brougham. Lyndhurst, when asked how he chose judges, is said to have answered, 'I look about for a gentleman, and if he knows a little law, so much the better.' On another occasion he was asked whether he believed in platonic friendships with ladies. 'After, but not before', was his answer. Brougham made his name in 1816 over a case for infringement of patent of a 'spinning jenny'. He went up to Nottingham, mastered the details of the machine so he could then operate one in court, and ended proving it was the plaintiffs who were guilty of infringement. Walter

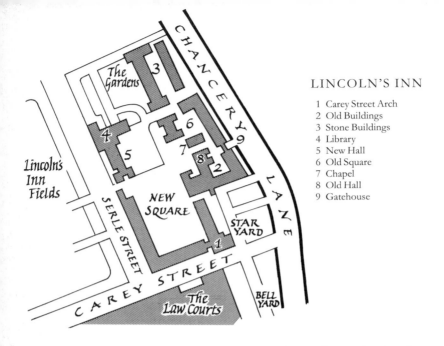

LINCOLN'S INN

1 Carey Street Arch
2 Old Buildings
3 Stone Buildings
4 Library
5 New Hall
6 Old Square
7 Chapel
8 Old Hall
9 Gatehouse

Bagehot, the great Victorian journalist and constitutional expert, commented on the look in Brougham's eye: 'If he were a horse, nobody would buy him.'

Later, there were three generations of the Russell family – a Lord Chief Justice followed by two Lords of Appeal – and Sir Frank Lockwood who prosecuted Oscar Wilde and defended the notorious murderer Charlie Peace without fee. Someone congratulating him on his defence, even though Peace was inevitably found guilty, called it 'Peace with Honour'. Lockwood accepted the compliment, but added, 'it was not peace at any price'.

Philip Hardwick's **New Hall** and **Library** are to the north of the cruet-set gateway by his son. Begun in 1843, these are excellent of their kind, a last flourish of the Picturesque before high Victorian earnestness and the quest for authenticity took over. Inside the Hall there is much heraldry, a hammer-beam roof and a fresco of ' The Lawgivers' by that titanic failure of an artist, G. F. Watts, 'England's Michelangelo'. Beyond it are the **Gardens**, open at lunchtime, guarded by an elaborate garden shed designed by no less than Sir George Gilbert Scott. He worked on extensions to the Library and built Jacobethan ranges to the north-east of the Chapel, which only go to show how good Hardwick's work in a

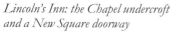
Lincoln's Inn: the Chapel undercroft and a New Square doorway

similar vein is. If you are a lawn fancier, these are reputed to be among England's best. To the east of the gardens, amongst all this diapered brickwork, comes **Stone Buildings** (1780) by Sir Robert Taylor, though the south end was handsomely added by Hardwick in the 1840s. There is a piquant little alley-way out of the north-east corner of Stone Buildings, worth penetrating if only to peer through the glass door of 76a Chancery Lane at its end. There you will see, descending to the basement bar and mess of the South East Circuit, a grand marble staircase round the newel post of which curls a large stone python.

The **Chapel**, open 12.00 to 2.30, is one of the many buildings round England no longer attributed to Inigo Jones. Its foundation stone was laid by the metaphysical poet and divine, John Donne, in 1620. He was preacher to the Inn from 1616 to 1622 and came back in 1623 to give the inaugural sermon in the chapel, when 'two or three were endangered and taken up dead for the time, with the extreme press and thronging'. The most striking aspects of the interior are the Jacobean pews, surviving from this time together with some stained glass. The bell, tolled whenever a bencher dies, is booty from the siege of Cadiz in 1596, brought back by the Earl of Essex. As one of the two most famous prose quotations by Donne (thanks to Ernest Hemingway) puts it: 'Never send to know for whom the bell tolls; it tolls for thee.' The open **Under-croft** was a good wet-weather meeting place for barristers, clerks and attorneys, and in 1659 eighty men who had been Members of the 'Rump' of the Long Parliament, finally dissolved by Oliver Cromwell in 1653, met here to plot the restoration of Charles II as King. Sometimes babies were abandoned here, and the Inn then took it on itself to bring them up, giving them the surname Lincoln. Any speculation that President Lincoln was descended from one such is enjoyable, but probably idle.

Cromwell is said to have lived in the **Gatehouse**, which was totally demolished before being rebuilt in the 1960s, though the gates themselves are original. The **Old Hall** is to be venerated, not merely as the lawyers' oldest building, but also for the inspiration it gave Dickens. It is typical of so many collegiate halls that followed it, with its screen at one end. But what is peculiar to it is a very indifferent painting by Hogarth, of St Paul before Felix, and the fact it has four bay windows. In the south-east one are assembled the arms of all those Inn members who have been Prime Ministers, except Margaret Thatcher, though both she and the Labour leader Tony Blair are honorary benchers of the Inn, whilst Mrs Cherie Blair is an active barrister member. Now that Lady Thatcher has been granted her coat of arms, complete with Captain Birdseye supporters, perhaps it will join the others. Benjamin Disraeli had chambers in **Old Buildings** before he abandoned law for novels and Parliament.

From 1737 to 1875 the Lord Chancellor held his High Court of Chancery in Old Hall out of term time. Thus it became, as the setting for the trial of Jarndyce versus Jarndyce, a vital ingredient of *Bleak House*, almost as important as the 'London particular . . . a fog, Miss'. The book's opening is as famous as the Donne quotation above, but can stand another airing: 'London. Michaelmas Term lately over, and the Lord Chancellor sitting in Lincoln's Inn Hall. Implacable November weather . . . Fog everywhere.'

Pump, garden gates and gardener, New Square

Dickens regarded this court as 'the most pestilent of hoary sinners', particularly in matters of probate, and wasn't prepared to see that some of the fault might lie with those who failed to make their wills clear. There is a nice irony in the fact that his own will became the subject of Chancery proceedings in 1934. He had left his private papers to his sister-in-law and his copyrights to his children. When his *Life of Christ* was published for the first time, to whom should the proceeds go? After deliberating the court ruled that half went to the sister-in-law's beneficiaries, who owned the manuscript of the book, and half to the descendants of Dickens.

Dickens had in fact worked for a few weeks as a clerk, aged 14, for the solicitor Charles Molloy at number 4, **New Square**, before he moved on to Gray's Inn. New Square is anything but, having started life in about 1685, not even as part of the Inn, rather as a speculative development by one of the benchers, Henry Serle. As so often happens to his kind, Serle went bankrupt in the process, but seems to have been forgiven since the street behind the west side of the square bears his name. Even now, not all the freehold of the Square belongs to the Inn. How splendid if the benchers were suddenly to go all green and order the removal of cars from around its central trees and lawn, so that its mellow ranges of brick could be seen to best advantage. Solicitors cluster thickly here, and indeed the whole of the south side is filled by Trowers and Hamlins, or trousers and hemlines if you wish to be facetious. Wildy's law bookshop has occupied what were the pavements on either side of the **Gateway** arch here since 1830. On 18th June 1832, the seventeenth anniversary of the Battle of Waterloo, the Duke of Wellington was forced to take refuge behind this gate from a mob that had pursued him all the way from Tower Hill. It was a few days after the passing of the Great Reform Bill, a measure to which he was opposed.

Leaving Lincoln's Inn through the gateway, you will emerge 'in **Carey Street**', home of the bankruptcy courts and hence another name for that condition. By turning right you can inspect the Silver Mousetrap silver shop, established 1690, the Seven Stars pub claiming to date from 1602, and finally Sir Thomas More Chambers. These are all parasitic outgrowths from the back of New Square, the last decorated with some good 'green men' bas reliefs,

Carey Street: Sir Thomas More Chambers, left, and the back of the Law Courts; right: The Silver Mousetrap

as well as the statue of More at first-floor level. Now retrace your steps, as you do so looking across the road at the back of the Law Courts, more Italianate in feel than the rest, with the horizontal bands of brick and stone making it look like one of those glass columns filled with coloured sands from Alum Bay in the Isle of Wight. There is no let-up in the quality and invention compared to the front (see p. 54). The only matter for regret is the choice of tree planted on the pavement here – are they dawn redwoods or swamp cypresses or what?

Past the Lincoln's Inn gateway once more, number 60 Carey Street is a distinguished double-fronted Georgian house (1732) with shutters to its ground-floor windows and a good – but later – door-frame. Residence of the President of the Law Society (see next paragraph) during his year's term of office, it is on the corner of **Star Yard**, home to one of London's few pissoirs, sadly now out of commission and with its entrance welded up. There are what appear to be stylised Japanese chrysanthemum motifs on it, which perhaps date it to the 1870s or 1880s and allow it to be claimed as a manifestation of the Aesthetic Movement. In *Bleak House* Krook maintained his rag-and-bottle warehouse here, until he sponta-neously combusted. The other corner of Star Yard is occupied by the Union Bank of London (1865 – now NatWest), a true temple to Mammon with its pairs of columns on the Chancery Lane side and pairs of pilasters on the Carey Street side, all obeying the rules as to the correct sequence of classical orders.

Turn right into **CHANCERY LANE** and, for the moment only look at what is on the west side. There is a remarkable run of buildings from this point down to Fleet Street. First comes the **Law Society**, the professional body of the solicitors. The original Greek Ionic building (1831) by Lewis Vulliamy comes across as calm, well proportioned and authoritative, presenting the profes-sion as it would wish to be seen. The extension (1902) by Charles Holden is a more exciting exercise in an angular classical style which yet manages to complement the main building. But cannot the terrible floodlights sticking out at first-floor level be banished? Number 114, what was the **Law Fire Insurance Office** by Thomas Bellamy, has been called 'one of the most refined Renaissance buildings of the mid-Victorian years' (G. Stamp and

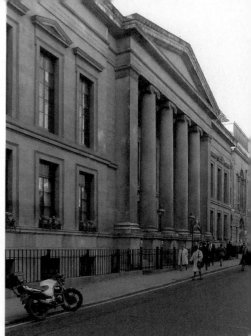

Chancery Lane: Hodgson's, once auction rooms, now wine bar; and The Law Society

C. Amery, *Victorian Buildings of London*). It looks unloved at the moment, but do not let the grime put you off examining the carved firemen's helmets either side of the door. If you have enjoyed these, you might even take yourself round to the back of the building in Bell Yard, where you will find more helmets, this time with crossed hatchets, and two very small firemen's heads in the left-hand capitals.

Pevsner dismisses as 'worthless' number 115, formerly **Hodgson's** book auction rooms and now a wine bar, but one can still enjoy the turbaned and bearded heads on the keystones, and the central wreathed female between two couchant, winged bat-dogs. Number 123–4, the Midland bank, is good Ruskinian Gothic from the first floor up, while number 125–6, Wheeler's Restaurant – sandstone and pink stucco – has some shapely caryatides supporting bishops' mitres, of all things. This sequence ends with number 193 Fleet Street, **Attenboroughs the Jewellers**. Polished Aberdeen granite below and red sandstone above, the shop was rebuilt in 1884 when Fleet Street was widened. There is a splendid series of carved roundels of the heads of all the artists whom the

Victorians worshipped – Raphael, Dürer, etc – at first-floor level, and a rather effete statue of the character Khaled from Byron's poem 'Lara':

> They were no common links that formed the chain
> That bound to Lara Khaled's heart and brain.

(The business used to specialize in 'Alberts' – gold watch chains.) The two fine gryphons (traditional guardians of gold) used to have the three gold balls of a pawnbroker's sign suspended between them, for Attenboroughs once combined that with their present business. Go into the shop because the original 1884 fixtures are still there and should not be missed.

Follow the pavement round, right, into Fleet Street and you will pass the former **Bank of England, Law Courts Branch** by Sir Arthur Blomfield (1888). Externally it is still a temple to the greater glory of money, but internally it is now a pub and its new owners have not done it any favours, though they have tried hard. Once you are past the Temple Bar pedestal in the middle of the

Left: Part of the south front of the Law Courts with perhaps London's most ornate lamp standard in the foreground
Right: the City dragon at Temple Bar, in front of the old Law Courts branch of the Bank of England

road (see p. 77) you have left the City and are in the Strand, with
the clock of the **ROYAL COURTS OF JUSTICE** sticking out
above you. This is the clock immortalized by P. G. Wodehouse in
his story 'Bertie Changes his Mind', to be found in *Carry On, Jeeves.*
At no notice Bertie Wooster is called upon to address a girls'
school and all he can come up with by way of advice to help them
through life is: 'If you stand outside Romano's in the Strand, you
can see the clock on the wall of the Law Courts . . . You can win a
lot of money betting on it with fellows who haven't found it out.'
Romano's Restaurant was at number 399, the Strand, well on the
way to Charing Cross, but Bertie is absolutely right.

The old law courts beside Westminster Hall were too small and
inefficient by the 1860s so a competition for a new building was
mounted. All the great names of the day entered – Scott, Street,
Waterhouse, Burges, Seddon, E. M. Barry – and the judging was
the shambles that such things always seem to be. G. E. Street
eventually was chosen, for many the greatest of the High Victorian exponents of Gothic. William Morris and Philip Webb (p. 13)
had worked in his offices. Street was much taken up with detail,
not very good at delegating and working to a very restricted
budget; the strain of producing the huge complex of the Law
Courts killed him in 1881, but the building, begun in 1871 and
opened in 1882, is his masterpiece.

The polychrome Italian Gothic elements detectable in the rear
have already been noted on page 51, but the overall style is north
European thirteenth-century Gothic, and what could be better
for impressing on all concerned the full majesty of the Law? The
standard criticism of the Strand elevation is that it is bitty, but
given the narrowness of the street it is not possible to see the
whole, so any attempt at an all-embracing treatment would have
been a waste of effort. Before going in, enjoy the subtle and
assured articulation of the Gothic grammar and vocabulary, both
on the south front and on the east and west sides, as well as much
carved foliage – ballflower, stiff-leaf, etc. – the ironwork and the
picturesque skyline. Once through the metal detectors (no pho-
tography or indeed cameras allowed inside), the **Hall** opens out
before you. This noble waste of space, 230 feet long and 82 feet
high, must often put the fear of God as well as dread of the law

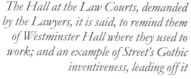

The Hall at the Law Courts, demanded by the Lawyers, it is said, to remind them of Westminster Hall where they used to work; and an example of Street's Gothic inventiveness, leading off it

into those about to set out for one of the dozens of courts leading off it. The rib vaulting soars, the highly polished tile and mosaic floor stretches out. Street is seated to the right, with his plans forming an apron across his knees. At the far end there is a good bronze bust of Queen Victoria by Alfred Gilbert, with more high quality vaulting beyond her, before you come to the café (there used to be a bar in the Crypt).

Down the centre of the Hall are glass cases with the lists of the day's trials in them. Take your pick, or consult one of the attendants as to which might prove most interesting. Remember that you will not find any big criminal cases here, with the full panoply of trial by jury. These are held at the Old Bailey, the Central Criminal Court, a short walk eastwards from Holborn Viaduct. The Law Courts are confined to Civil cases and Appeals, but with a bit of luck even these can make for fascinating listening. At certain points a trial may be closed to the public, in which case a sign on the door will make this clear. Otherwise, the back two rows of

seats are for the public's use, so set out up one of the spiral stairs
and down the corridors to find the court of your choice.

The original courts come up to expectations: spacious, with
lots of dark wood, rows of leather-bound volumes of law reports,
high ceilings and much variation of floor level. There may be
washing lines with microphones hanging from them and the clerk
will probably have a lap-top, but wigs are still worn. You have
ample time to study their construction as you survey the backs of
the barristers in front of you, their formalized curls looking like
pallid canapés or wood shavings. One impression is the quantity
of paperwork – stacks, folders and files full of it – that the barristers and their solicitors bring to court. But with luck the judge
won't be stifling a yawn or playing with a piece of string to relieve
his understandable boredom, and you will forget the surround-
ings, absorbed instead by the arguments; you will marvel at the
skills displayed, and be impressed by the great pains taken to see
justice done. If you are not, rise to your feet, nod respectfully to
the judge, and find another trial down the corridor.

Go back along the north side of the Strand and then Fleet
Street, cross Chancery Lane and turn in next left up **Clifford's
Inn** Passage. In *Our Mutual Friend* Dickens has Mr Boffin glance
'into the mouldy little plantation, or cat-preserve of Clifford's Inn .
. . Sparrows were there, dry-rot and wet-rot were there, but it was
not otherwise a suggestive spot.' Things have not changed: all that
remains of this Inn of Chancery is the gateway ahead, the rest of
the largely eighteenth-century buildings having been demolished
as recently as 1935. Samuel Butler, that inveterate deflater and the
author of *Erewhon*, lived here from 1864 until his death in 1902. In
his wonderful *Notebooks* he confirmed Dickens' observation.
'People, when they want to get rid of their cats and do not like
killing them, bring them to the garden of Clifford's Inn, drop
them there, and go away.'

Once through the gateway, head for the fig tree in front of you.
Behind the tree can be seen the remains of the chancel arch from
the old Rolls Chapel, demolished to make way for the **Public
Records Office**. Left at the tree, right up Chancery Lane to the
PRO gateway. Henry III founded a house on this site for Jewish
converts, but his son Edward I then expelled all Jews from

John Wilkes

One of the Public Record Office's pepperpots, with the 1902 extension to the Law Society

England in 1290. In the next century the Keeper of the Rolls of Chancery (documents and records written on parchment scrolls) moved in. In 1851–66 the Fetter Lane end of the present building was constructed by Sir James Pennethorne, purpose-built with a cast-iron frame, ceilings made from brick arches and storage shelves from slate: for this was to be the collective memory of the nation and these materials were a precaution against Fahrenheit 451 degrees, the temperature at which paper combusts. Beneath the decorative crust of pierced parapets and perpendicular pepperpots, the regular structure proclaims the high seriousness of the enterprise. The Chancery Lane side, to the west of the central tower with its statues of English queens, was added in 1891–6. But what is going to happen to it all now? From the autumn of 1995 the PRO will start to move out, to go and join its newer deposits already located at Kew – so convenient.

For the moment you can still visit the small museum and see an infinitesimal and changing sample of the holdings: the Doomsday

Book; the Lord Chamberlain's pattern book, open at a page of samples for the gold lace of Royal Household trumpeters in 1824; the Golden Bull of 1521 sent to Henry VIII by Pope Leo X, bestowing the title of Defender of the Faith in recognition of his attack on Luther; Nelson's passing certificate on becoming a Lieutenant in 1777. In the original museum room on the other side of the corridor, with handsome perpendicular windows full of heraldic stained glass, there are three monuments rescued from the old Rolls Chapel. The earliest is to Dr Yonge, Master of the Rolls (d. 1516) and is by Pietro Torrigiano, a Florentine who was a fellow-student with Michelangelo in the art school set up by Lorenzo de' Medici. He had a fight with Michelangelo, broke his nose, and fled to Rome before coming to England to sculpt the tomb of Henry VII and his wife, and also that of Henry's mother, in Westminster Abbey. His was the first visual impress of the Renaissance on England, and a detail such as the head of Christ above the recumbent Doctor must have had an arresting effect. (There is also a bronze profile of Sir Thomas Lovell, he of Lincoln's Inn gatehouse (p. 44), by Torrigiano in the Abbey.) Next comes Richard Alington of Lincoln's Inn (d. 1561), kneeling in armour opposite his wife, with their three ruffed daughters below and two grotesque faces garlanded by fruit above. Lastly, Lord Bruce (d 1611), recumbent, leaning on his elbow in the pose ridiculed by Webster in *The Duchess of Malfi*, 'as if they died o' the toothache'. But he looks more comfortable than his four kneeling children below, the girls with ruffs at neck and waist, farthingales and alarming hairdos.

Turn right out of the PRO and continue northwards, up **Chancery Lane**. Number 93 is Ede and Ravenscroft's shop, open for the purchase of wigs and gowns. Number 87 is a polychrome Gothic gem (1863) by Arthur Blomfield. Turn right down **Bream's Buildings**, where number 5 has blue-and-white tiled pilasters and jolly plasterwork satyrs and nymphs under the cornice, and number 11 is more quality Gothic. You will get a good view of the east side of the PRO from Fetter Lane at the end of Bream's Buildings, and of a new (1988) statue of that attractive rogue and key player in the political scene after 1760, **John Wilkes**. In appearance he was startlingly ugly, with a ferocious

Ede and Ravenscroft's shop window: barristers' wigs to the left, judges' centre, and judicial braces right

squint, but it is said he could 'talk away his face in half an hour'. The squint is there in the statue, but for the rest it is rather bland.

Go left, northwards up Fetter Lane for a few yards, before diving, left, into Greystoke Place, which leads to Cursitor Street, off which is **Took's Court**. Numbers 14 and 15 with their brick pilasters are very pleasing early eighteenth-century houses, number 15 being called Dickens' House, no doubt because in *Bleak House*, Mr Snagsby the law stationer lived here, though Dickens called it Cooks Court. Mrs Snagsby was 'the high standard of comparison among the neighbouring wives, a long way down Chancery Lane on both sides', whilst Mr Snagsby 'dealt in all sorts of blank forms of legal process, in skins and rolls of parchment, in paper — foolscap, brief, draft, brown, white, whitey-brown, and blotting; in stamps, office quills, pens, ink, India rubber, pounce, pins, pencils, sealing wax and wafers; in red tape and green ferret; in pocket books, almanacks, diaries and Law lists; in string, boxes, rulers, inkstands (glass and leaden), penknives, scissors, bodkins, and other office cutlery.' The concrete structure, with two ventila-

Left: Chancery Lane and a Lincoln's Inn window seen through the aperture of Quality Court. Right: Staple Inn courtyard

tion shafts, round the corner in Took's Court is, one hopes, the former London Centre of Regional Government. These supposedly nuclear-attack-proof bunkers were built in the 1950s to house those who would keep the administration going after the Bomb.

Back to Chancery Lane and northward past Quality Court to the corner of Southampton Buildings, on which stand the **London Silver Vaults** – they close at lunchtime on Saturdays – where hundreds of toast-racks and teapots are looking for a good home. The Vaults began as a Safe Deposit, but after 1945 more and more silver dealers set up in them. Now there are about forty, offering the biggest collection under one roof in the world. Go down Southampton Buildings, past the **Patent Office**, guardian of intellectual property, and through the wrought iron gates at the end, which open onto the garden of **Staple Inn**. It sports a fountain, a fig and a catalpa, and you can walk through it to the cobbled courtyard of this Inn of Chancery, now the home of the Institute of Actuaries. What you see – the Hall and the Georgian chambers – are largely a recreation, for they were hit by a flying bomb in 1944.

Staple Inn garden

In 1759 Dr Johnson lived here after leaving Gough Square (p. 106) and wrote his tale *Rasselas* in a week: the money earned went to pay for his mother's funeral. In *Edwin Drood* Dickens called it 'one of those nooks, the turning into which out of the clashing street, imparts to the relieved pedestrian the sensation of having put cotton in his ears, and velvet soles on his boots'. Certainly as you go through the archway out into Holborn, the noise assaults you.

Turn right along Holborn, looking up at the half-timbered fronts of the Inn buildings. These, familiar from the Old Holborn tobacco packet, are genuine, though the buildings behind the facade have been reconstructed (1937). You soon come to **Dyer's Buildings**, a long, thin Victorian court, paved with York stone, with a good display of busy lizzies and allowing a fine, framed view of the tower of the Pru Building on the other side of Holborn. Next take the passageway that leads to **Barnard's Inn**, the other Inn of Chancery besides Staple Inn to be associated with Gray's Inn. It began life as Macworth's Inn (he was a medieval Dean of Lincoln). By the nineteenth century it had gone downhill, and Dickens described it in *Great Expectations* as 'the dingiest set of

Left: The Pru framed by the narrow inlet of Dyers Buildings
Right: The fire escape by Barnard's Inn

buildings ever squeezed together in a rank corner as a club for
tom-cats'. In the 1890s it was taken over as the new premises of
the Mercers' School from further east in the City. The Hall was
preserved until 1931, when decay forced a replica to be built, but
using quite a lot of old material. The school eventually closed in
1959 and the site has very recently been redeveloped. The Hall is
so small that it is easy to miss. One's eye is distracted by an amazing post-modern fire escape, painted dark khaki, looming above it.
This end of the site is now the home of Gresham College (p. 28),
but proceed, through the satisfying new dog-legged stone passage
with Doric columns at either end, into a less successful new court
of looming offices. The ingredients - golden and red brick, stone,
black Doric columns and black roundels - all rather fight each
other for attention. Carry on past the Mercury Communications
offices out into Fetter Lane and turn left. Here at **number 80** has
survived the most enchanting sandstone facade in the Gothic/Art
Nouveau/Arts-and-Crafts style, covered with carvings of considerable accomplishment – winged masks at first floor level, green

men at the second and third floors, and seated, cross-legged atlantes at the top. Dated 1902, it is by Treadwell and Martin (who did a number of equally delightful shop fronts in the West End) and presumably associated with their now-demolished Buchanan's distillery building on the corner of Fetter Lane and Holborn. This was the successor to the Catholic-owned Langdale's distillery, the destruction of which, in the Gordon Riots of 1780, forms one of Dickens' great setpieces in *Barnaby Rudge*. 'From the burning cellars, where they drank out of hats, pails, buckets, tubs and shoes, some men were drawn alive, but all alight from head to foot; who, in their unendurable anguish and suffering, making for anything that had the look of water, rolled, hissing, in this hideous lake, and splashed up liquid fire which lapped in all it met with. . .' It makes a fitting finale to this section, before you emerge into Holborn again, to walk back to Chancery Lane tube.

A carving on number 80, Fetter Lane

WALK THREE

The Middle Temple, the Embankment, and the Strand to Somerset House

When you emerge from Temple tube (closed on Sundays) turn left, westwards along Temple Place and past the green-painted taxi cabbies' rest, then right up Surrey Street. Amongst the terracotta frontages of the old Norfolk Hotel, halfway up on the left, is Surrey Steps passageway. Once in Strand Lane at the foot of the steps turn right to discover what must be the National Trust's smallest property, the **Roman Bath**. It is probably not Roman but *is* old, and was patronized by David Copperfield. Fed by a spring giving 2000 gallons a day, it can be seen by switching on the light and looking through the window. Next to it, arching across the alley, is the old **Watch House** belonging to the parish watch of St Clement Danes Church, dignified by an elegant Trafalgar balcony.

Bravura terracotta columns of the old Norfolk Hotel in Surrey Street: flowers, fruit, a mask at the top and entwined Chinoiserie ho-ho birds at the bottom

Late-Victorian wrought ironwork in front of the old Astor Estate office, Temple Place

WALK THREE

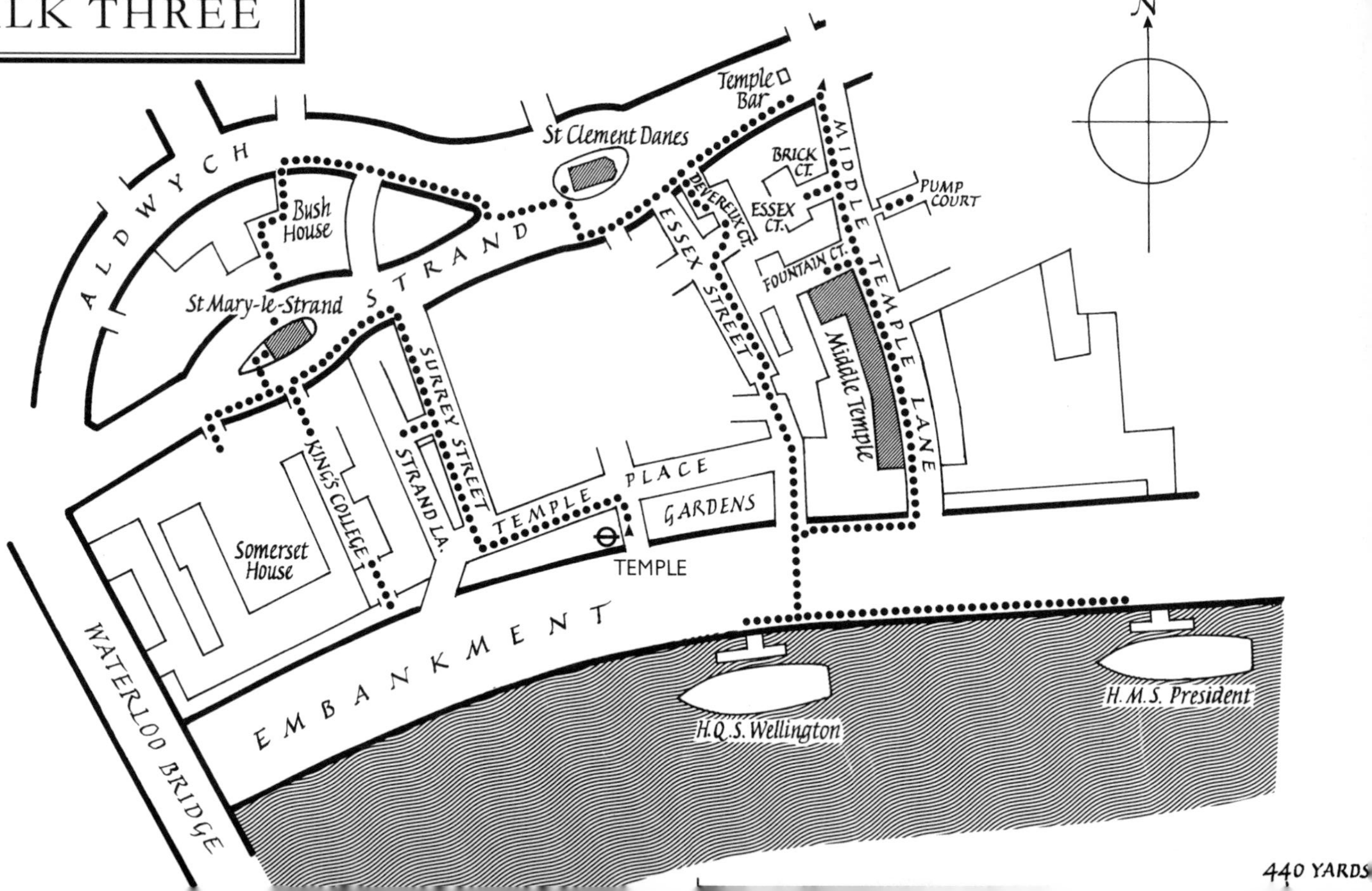

440 YARDS

N

Temple Bar
St Clement Danes
ALDWYCH
STRAND
Bush House
St Mary-le-Strand
PUMP COURT
MIDDLE TEMPLE LANE
Middle Temple
BRICK CT.
ESSEX CT.
FOUNTAIN CT.
DEVEREUX CT.
ESSEX STREET
TEMPLE PLACE
GARDENS
TEMPLE
SURREY STREET
STRAND LA.
KING'S COLLEGE
Somerset House
EMBANKMENT
WATERLOO BRIDGE
H.M.S. President
H.Q.S. Wellington

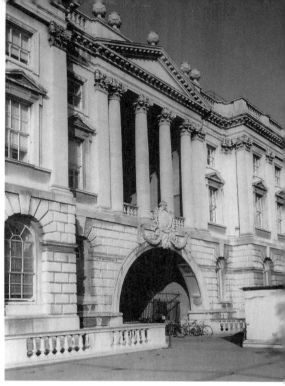

Left: bridge of sighs connecting King's College to its Surrey Street buildings. Right: the eastern Palladian bridge at the end of the College courtyard, viewed from the terrace above the Thames

From it no doubt there is a good view, down the hill, of the apse of King's College Chapel sticking out in mid-air, supported on cast-iron pillars, and two bridges of sighs for the students to come and go, but whether talking of Michelangelo one is less sure, in spite of his proximity (p. 73).

Back into Surrey Street and on up to the **STRAND**, then left past the shiny ox-blood-coloured tiles of Aldwych tube station, on a branch line which was finally shut down in 1994. It is the scene of one of the high points in Geoffrey Household's great pre-war thriller, *Rogue Male*. The hero's attempt to shoot Hitler has failed, and now, trying to shake off his pursuers on the Underground, he is cornered by one of them in the dead-end tunnel here:

Aldwych Station is deserted as an ancient mine. You can hear the drip of water and the beat of your heart.

I can still hear them, and the sound of steps and his scream and the hideous, because domestic, sound of sizzling.

The entrance to **King's College**, University of London, is past it on the left. This area has a high student density because the Courtauld Institute, the History of Art faculty of the University, is in Somerset House next door, while the London School of Economics is the other side of Aldwych, a few yards to the north. Walk to the end of King's courtyard, with Smirke's 1835 range on the left and the back of Chambers' eastern Somerset House range to the right. The latter gives the effect of having a series of doors down its length, until one comes closer and sees the vertiginous area separating it from the courtyard. Go underneath the arch of the elegant Palladian bridge at the end and you find yourself on the terrace of Somerset House at treetop level, with a good view up and down the river, which originally lapped the giant arched water gates below.

Back to the front door of the Smirke block, up the stairs to the first floor and into the **Chapel**, by Sir George Gilbert Scott (1872). As startling a church interior and as pleasant a surprise as you could ask for, it is an essay in Romano-Byzantine, its round arches supported on kingfisher-blue cast-iron double columns, with what looks like marquetry at clerestory level. Athanasius, Basil, Chrysostom, Ambrose and Augustine appear in roundels on one side, with Jerome, Gregory, Hooker, Andrews, Taylor and Pearson on the other, leaving no room for doubt about the Catholic descent of the Anglican Church. King's College was, after all, founded as a counterweight to the 'godless' University College up in Bloomsbury, which was intended for non-Anglicans. You will need to have topped up your spiritual reserves here to face the brutalism of the north range of King's (1971) which will hit you as you head for the Strand. Avert your eyes quickly to the left for a vista of Somerset House through Chambers' arch there.

Once back in the Strand, before you, islanded in a sea of westbound traffic, stands **St Mary-le-Strand**. We owe it to a change of government from Whig to Tory in 1710. To celebrate their return from many years in the political wilderness the Tories, who saw themselves pre-eminently as the champions of the Anglican Church, passed an Act for the building of fifty churches, to be financed by a tax on coal. Nothing like that number got built, but it gave Hawksmoor his head, mostly further east, and James Gibbs his chance here (1717). By a nice irony, the Scottish Gibbs was in

St Mary-le-Strand; and Somerset House vestibule, Strand block.

fact a covert Roman Catholic and had gone to Rome originally to train for the priesthood. Instead he became infected by the spirit of Baroque, which, when crossed with various themes from Wren's St Paul's, produced the winner here before you. It is safest to admire his use of niches and varied pediments on the sides before crossing the road and entering the tiny patch of garden through the gates with their eroded putti. Beyond the ginkgos and magnolias is a delightful semi-circular flight of steps and porch, with the spire (a late but very happy thought) above it. Inside one is surprised by the comparative quiet, until it dawns that the windows only start at first floor level. Dickens' parents were married here in 1809, handy for his father who was a clerk in the Navy Office in Somerset House. Outside, on the south side of the pedestal on which the building stands, can still be seen the vault numbers of those buried beneath the thundering traffic. It is hard to believe, but in the early 1980s St Mary was under threat of demolition. Many sprang to its defence, including John Betjeman, who composed verses beginning:

Somerset House: one of Chambers' twin arches, with Smirke's King's College range beyond; Father Thames points a languid finger in the courtyard

Shall we give Gibbs the go-by
Great Gibbs of Aberdeen

If you walk a little westwards down the Strand from here, the tip-top of the spire of Gibbs' other triumph, St Martin-in-the-Fields, can be seen over the roof-tops, as can Nelson on his column. Equally, if you look back eastwards you will see the cover design for the old *Strand Magazine*, sacred as the birthplace of so many of the Sherlock Holmes stories.

SOMERSET HOUSE, designed by Sir William Chambers and begun in 1776, is on the site of the house built by Protector Somerset, effective ruler of England during the reign of the boy king, Edward VI. It was to serve two purposes: to house a string of government departments including the Navy Office (by far the biggest), Exchequer, Privy Seal, Audit, and Duchy of Cornwall; and to house the newly founded Royal Academy of Arts, the scientific Royal Society founded by Charles II, and the Society of Antiquaries – precursors of today's archaeologists. The range facing the Strand was where these societies were to congregate, but an aquatic note is struck straight away in the keystones to the rusticated arcade, bearded heads representing the ocean in the centre and eight English rivers. The four 'venerable men' at the top are Justice (scales), Prudence (mirror), Valour (sword) and Moderation (bridle).

It is customary to damn Somerset House with faint praise, but there are elements in it which easily escape any charge of mere competence, such as the vestibule you pass through to the great courtyard beyond. It is a satisfying scheme of coupled columns, providing elegant entrances to the learned societies on either side. The south courtyard frontage of the Strand range is a variation of the northern, with pilasters instead of columns, and statues of the Four Continents. An unrecognisable bronze statue of a toga'd George III, his left arm resting on the steering oar from a classical galley, confronts you; below him is an allegorical Father Thames, his left arm draped with his water-logged beard (John Bacon, 1789).

The courtyard behind them labours under the huge disadvantage of being used as a car park by the employees of the Inland Revenue, the occupants of most of the surrounding buildings now. Civil servants' cars look like being swept away from Horse Guards Parade by St James's Park. Why not here too? For the rest, the extension of the rustication up to the second floor does not seem very happy, and the two domed clock lanterns look inadequate. In the centre the coloured stone flags on Lutyens' war memorial to that apparent contradiction, the Civil Service Rifles, are also a mistake. The southern range overlooking the river houses the Principal Registry of the Family Division of the High Court. All is not as it seems for above the balustrade the attic, pediment and drum below the copper dome are made of wood.

Do not omit to look into one of the areas, revealing two more storeys below the courtyard level, and giving off something of a *Gormenghast*, Piranesian, or even Kafkaesque exhalation, with its flights of steps, walkways and bridges. Go also through the western arch (twin to that on the King's College side), past the former Hawkers and Pedlars Office, and look down the vista formed by Sir James Pennethorne's 1856 range, not only to the Palladian

The western Palladian bridge, beyond a Victorian interloper

bridge (twin to that on the King's College side), but also to an interloping utilitarian Victorian bridge in the foreground. They make a bizarre pairing.

Passing through what was the Royal Academy's doorway, under the bust of Michelangelo, you enter the newish home of the **Courtauld Institute Galleries** and are immediately greeted by two cheery centaurs. Even if you have no time for the galleries, go up the steps between the greeters so that you can look up, and down, the intriguing semicircular stairwell. The stagey facade added below was an unsuccessful attempt to reconcile the Keeper of the RA to his basement flat. The Institute, founded in 1930, was the brainchild of the collector Lord Lee of Fareham, who had already given Chequers to the nation, to be a country house for the Prime Minister. The money, however, came from the collector and textile magnate Samuel Courtauld, rich from the profits of rayon, the new artificial fibre. From 1932 to 1989 the Institute was in Portman Square.

At the centre of the collection in the galleries are the Impressionists and post-Impressionists bought by Courtauld. The star of the

The repeated curves of Chambers' staircase up to what were the Royal Academy's rooms and are now the Courtauld Galleries

show is Manet's *Bar at the Folies-Bergère*, well stocked with a bowl of tangerines, bottles of Bass, champagne, crème de menthe, and what looks like some rosé; the barmaid with her fringe and amazing waist, wearing a corsage and a locket on a black ribbon round her neck. The more melancholy side of Paris comes over in Toulouse-Lautrec's portrait of Jane Avril pulling on her gloves outside the Moulin Rouge, her prognathous jaw disappearing into her fur.

The other two major holdings are those from Lord Lee and from Count Anton Seilern, who came to live in England in 1939. His gift, known as the Prince's Gate Collection, is notable for its pictures by Rubens and G. B. Tiepolo. Lord Lee's pictures range from the Flemish fourteenth century, through the Italian Renaissance, to the English eighteenth century; if two must be singled out, let them be Giovanni Bellini's *Assassination of St Peter Martyr* and William Dobson's *An Older and a Younger Man*, not a great but a moving, melancholic work, redolent of the sad times (1640s) in which it was painted.

It is not possible to say in which room any picture is because there seems to be a fairly constant rearrangement going on. The most easterly rooms on each floor were those used by the Royal Society and the Society of Antiquaries, whilst the big top-lit gallery on the second floor was the Royal Academy Great Room, used from 1780 to 1836 for the annual Summer Exhibition. The competition to be hung on or below the seven-foot high 'line', rather than 'skied' somewhere above it, was always fierce. The decorative schemes of the rooms are being restored to their original colourings and finishes where possible, to do justice to the plasterwork and chimney-pieces. In the process, let's hope the nasty peacock-blue labels on the doors and green illuminated exit signs above them can go. The fitted carpets are anachronistic and beginning to show the dirt, while the temporary air conditioning is noisy – a prime case for some National Lottery money.

Coming out of the Courtauld, you will see opposite you the doorway which served the Royal Society and the Antiquaries, with a bust of Newton above it. There is normally a special exhibition, of prints or drawings for instance, on this far side. Emerge into the Strand again for a look at **Bush House** on the Aldwych island, beyond St Mary. This island and the roadway separating it from the church were created as part of the Kingsway scheme in the 1900s. The curve given to the buildings turns them into a most satisfying frame for the church, which also benefits from its north side standing free of any clutter. The sculpture in the southern pediment of Bush House – a galleon in full sail in mid-Atlantic with lists of American and British Luminaries on either side – reminds that Irving T. Bush, the developer who carried out the Aldwych scheme, was an American. This is confirmed on its north front by symbolic figures of the US and Britain beneath the giant exedra. Bush House is now put to a thoroughly polyglot purpose as the home of the World Service of the BBC. To its west is **India House**, its balconies either flanked or supported by elephants and its third-floor balcony canopy decorated with multi-headed cobras. To its east is **Australia House** with some gruesome bronze statuary on the top of it – four prancing horses, which give an impression of being largely flaring nostrils, and a male figure, nude except for some sort of spiked halo. On the left of the door, among much other heavyweight allegory, is what must be one of the few carv-

Left: Bush House, which closes the vista down Kingsway, and is the home of the BBC World Service
Right: Bomber Harris with the spire of St Clement Danes

ings of a merino sheep. For some less plonking street sculpture look northwards across Aldwych here to number 99, **Clement House**: slightly obese putti, though with some feet missing, and two figures seated on the broken pediment above.

St Clement Danes was built by Wren in 1682, burnt out in 1941, and rebuilt in 1958 as the Royal Air Force church. It is not a very exciting space within, but filled with insignia, heraldry, love and pride and sadness, a palpable collective memory. The tower above the clock and the spire above that are Gibbs' work, but claims that the bells inside are those of the 'Oranges and Lemons' nursery rhyme are challenged by St Clement's Eastcheap. Outside, at its shrapnel-scarred east end, is a statue of Dr Johnson, which makes him look neckless and toadlike. Before the west front stand Dowding of Fighter Command and Harris of Bomber Command; not great statues, whatever the eventual reputations of the men portrayed. Lastly there is Thornycroft's group of Gladstone surrounded by Brotherhood, Aspiration, Education and Courage, who wears a leopard's mask on her head and is about to decapitate a snake with a scimitar. One is reminded irresistibly of Disraeli's jibe, that the trouble with Mr Gladstone was that he had not a single redeeming defect.

There was a cluster of Inns of Chancery hereabouts – **Lyon's** and **New** on the Aldwych island, **Strand** south of St Mary's and **Clement's** just to the north of St Clement's churches. All trace of them has long gone except that Clement's lives on in the lines given to Justice Shallow by Shakespeare in *Henry IV* Part 2: 'I was once of Clement's Inn; where I think they will talk of mad Shallow yet . . . There was I, and Little John Doit of Staffordshire, and black George Barnes, and Francis Pickbone, and Will Squele a Cotswold man; you had not four such swinge-bucklers in all the inns of court again . . .'

Walk along the south side of the Strand until you come to number 216, a white doorway with a golden lion and two comfortably seated, colourful Chinamen in the pediment above. These are the premises of **Twinings**, tea sellers here since the early eighteenth century. Tea is not served in the shop, but it is sold, every imaginable kind. The names alone make a fragrant invocation: Lapsang Souchong, Keemun, Oolong, Rose Pouchong, Yunnan, Russian Caravan, Darjeeling, Irish Breakfast, Assam. Buy some and look at Twining's small museum at the same time. In 1824 the Twining family diversified into banking, operating from number 215, but in the 1890s this side of their business was taken over by Lloyds Bank, which moved into number 222 Strand. **Lloyds Law Courts Branch** is far too much fun to have begun life as a bank, and indeed it did not. It was built in the 1880s as a restaurant, latterly called the Palsgrave after the Palsgrave Head Tavern which had been on the site in the seventeenth century. The Palsgrave was another name for Frederick, Elector Palatine whose marriage masques in 1613 were performed by members of the Inns of Court in such style (p. 16 and 45).

The entry vestibule is a riot of glazed majolica tile work, including columns, fish and cherubs. Inside there are handpainted Doulton tile panels of a variety of chrysanthemums and characters from the plays of Ben Jonson. The woodwork is American walnut and sequoia.

On the east side of Lloyds Law Courts Branch there is the answer to a question that many people ask – if there is an Inner and a Middle Temple, where is the **Outer Temple**? It is the office block just here, on land that belonged to the medieval Knights Templar but which is beyond Temple Bar. It is linked to Middle Temple's Essex Court by a bizarre glass-roofed passage lined with white-glazed tiles, for all the world like the entry to some long-lost public conveniences.

The prancing dragon on a plinth in the middle of the road marks the City boundary of **Temple Bar**. Its predecessor, the seventeenth-century stone archway, was removed in 1878 and re-erected in Theobalds Park in Essex where it sleeps, waiting for repair and a suitable new home, possibly to the north of St Paul's. Temple Bar was one of those spots, like old London Bridge, where the heads of traitors were exposed. The last two belonged to Jacobite officers executed after the 1745 rising. Horace Walpole recounts how there was much demand for telescopes hired out beside the Bar for a better view of them. Their remnants did not

Left: Temple Bar, Strand side, with Child's Bank to the right and Roger North's pedimented Middle Temple gateway building behind
Right: the old Astor Estate office in Temple Place

finally come down until 1772. The statues of Queen Victoria and
Edward VII as Prince of Wales below the dragon are by Sir Edgar
Boehm – he who died whilst making love to Edward's sister
Princess Louise in 1890, according to that reprobate Wilfrid
Scawen Blunt, who said he heard it from the great Victorian
courtesan Skittles (Catherine Walters), who had been told by the
Queen's physician, who had been involved in the cover-up.
Skittles had been kept by Edward VII and claimed he knew, too. If
the Sovereign visits the City she must stop and be met at this point
by the Lord Mayor, who proffers the City Sword, as can be seen in
a bas relief on the side of the plinth.

Beside Temple Bar are two tall, thin, white-painted houses,
home to the **Wig and Pen Club**, and dating from 1625. Could they
have witnessed Boswell with Johnson very shortly after they met,
in July 1763, when Johnson was living in the Temple? 'As we
walked along the Strand tonight, arm in arm, a woman of the town
came enticingly near us. "No," said Mr Johnson, "no, my girl,
it won't do." We then talked of the unhappy situation of these
wretches, and how much more misery than happiness, upon the
whole, is produced by irregular love.' Four nights later, Boswell was
in the Strand by himself: 'I was tapped on the shoulder by a fine
fresh lass. I went home with her.' Now he argued, 'Surely . . . when
the woman is already abandoned, the crime must be alleviated.'

Walk back until just past Twinings and turn into **Devereux
Court** by the George pub. This will lead you to the Devereux pub,
formerly the Grecian Coffee House, frequented in the eighteenth
century by Addison, Steele and many Fellows of the Royal Society
before or after their formal meetings in Crane Court off Fleet Street.
There is a gateway just by it into Middle Temple, but ignore it and
swing right, when two more pubs will be seen. The first is the Edgar
Wallace, named after that most prolific of authors who as a boy sold
papers at Ludgate Circus. His first book was *The Four Just Men*, in
1905. He died in 1932 having written 150 volumes in twenty-seven
years, largely to pay for his gambling. The second pub is called the
Cheshire Cheese, but is not to be confused with the more famous
Old Cheshire Cheese, further east down Fleet Street (p.104).

Turn left into **Essex Street**, developed by Nicholas Barbon
(see p. 88) between 1675 and 1682, on the site of Essex House,

home of the Devereux family, Earls of Essex. The most famous was Elizabeth's last great favourite, executed for treason in 1601. Another commanded the Parliamentary army early in the Civil War. On his clandestine, fleeting visit to London in 1750 Bonnie Prince Charlie is supposed to have stayed here, long enough to convert to the C. of E. in one of the new Strand churches and, presumably, to shudder at those heads of his followers on their poles above Temple Bar. Numbers 11, 14, 19 and 34 are original.

The arch at the south end of Essex Street was first built by Barbon to hide the commercial riverside wharves beyond. This ruse was not entirely successful, as some verses hint:

> In Essex Street, Strand, three attorneys have place,
> And three dusky coal barges are moored at the base.
> Fly, Honesty! Fly from this shady retreat
> For there's craft in the river and craft in the street.

> *The riposte*
> Why should Honesty fly from this shady retreat,
> From the lawyers and barges ('Od rot'em)?
> For the lawyers are just at the top of the street
> And the barges are just at the bottom.

The river has now retreated far from Essex Steps beneath the arch, thanks to Sir Joseph Bazalgette's embankment of it (1864–70). To the right (below a passage which rejoices in the name of Tweezer's Alley), in Temple Place, is the former **Astor Estate Office**, a Portland stone jewel box in Tudor style by J. L. Pearson (1895). The gilded weather vane is a large caravel with all sails set. Inside are said to be such things as a gallery of ebony columns and a door covered in silver gilt panels depicting 'Enid', 'Elaine' and others, by Sir George Frampton. To see something by Frampton at last, cross the **EMBANKMENT** road to the riverside where there is his **memorial to W. T. Stead**, a campaigning journalist who went down in the *Titanic*. Stead's greatest crusade was against child prostitution in London, 'the Maiden Tribute of Modern Babylon'. One cannot see the *Sun* coming up with a headline like that. The supporters on either side of Stead's portrait, though small, are worth study: Fortitude, a knight, and Sympathy, a woman.

Above: Sphinx and camel benches on the Embankment
Right: Statuary in Victoria Embankment Gardens

There are lots of incidental sculptural pleasures hereabouts, like the two bronze marine putti in front of H.Q.S. *Wellington*, floating livery hall for the Master Mariners' Company. Also look over the wall at the mooring rings clasped in lions' jaws, at the entwined dolphin lamp standards, and at the benches on pedestals with sphinx or kneeling camel ends. It would be logical if these had been designed to complement Cleopatra's Needle to the west, but they date from 1870 at the latest and the Needle was only erected in 1878. For serious statuary, cross back over the road and go into the pocket-handkerchief-sized **Victoria Embankment Gardens**. John Stuart Mill, philosopher, economist and early champion of the rights of women, comes first. Then there is a small girl proffering a bowl. She commemorates Lady Isabella Somerset, founder of the 'first industrial farm for inebriate women'. If you think the small girl doesn't have the patina of age about her you are right: the original was stolen in 1971, sawn off at the feet. Next there is W. E. Forster who in 1870 introduced the bill to set up elementary schools for all, to be paid for out of the rates and to work alongside the various church schools. Another Victorian worthy has, as it were, strayed westwards beyond Temple tube: Isambard Kingdom Brunel, builder of the Clifton suspension bridge, the Great Western Railway and the *Great Eastern* steamship. Like the other two men, he is visible

evidence of the difficulty sculptors have always had with trousers.

Temple Steps are now by the *Wellington*, but would have been further back before the building of the Embankment. In 1613 Thomas Hutchinson of Gray's Inn was attacked by his wicked guardian Sir Germaine Poole at the steps, 'who assaulting the other upon advantage, and cutting off two of his fingers . . . before he could draw, the gentleman [Hutchinson], finding himself disabled to revenge himself by the sword [Poole was wearing a mail shirt], flew in upon him and getting him down tore away all his eyebrow with his teeth, and then seizing on his nose bit off a good part of it and carried it away in his pocket' (Chamberlain).

Scott of the Antarctic's ship *Discovery* left its anchorage for Chatham some time ago and H.M.S. *Chrysanthemum* is also missing, but the other ship used by the educational charity Inter-Action Trust, H.M.S. *President*, is still here. If you walk towards her, you will come upon the Submarine War Memorial: four booted, square-jawed, submariners in roll-neck jerseys, surrounded by threatening spirits of the deep, together with the numbers or, in the case of the last war, the names of the vessels lost. There is a good view over the river to the Oxo Tower, the flash Sea Containers House, the new *Express* Newspapers office and Bankside Power Station beyond Blackfriars Bridge, due to become an outstation of the Tate Gallery.

Cross back over the Embankment road by the stern of the *Wellington* and go up Middle Temple Lane to E. M. Barry's extraordinary **Temple Gardens Building** of 1879. If one did not know of his busy career before this, designing the Royal Opera House in Covent Garden, the Charing Cross Hotel (one of Betjeman's favourite buildings), nearly getting the Law Courts job, one would suggest this was the work of a very recently qualified architect, previously a pastry cook, who had been much influenced by the chateaux of the Loire. But, if impossible to take seriously, it is easy to enjoy. The building is common to the Middle and to the Inner Temple which is why the former's Lamb and Flag badge and the latter's Pegasus or winged horse are either side of the arch:

> That clients may infer from thence,
> How just is their profession,
> The Lamb sets forth their innocence,
> The Horse their expedition.
> Oh happy Britons! Happy Isle!
> Let foreign nations say –
> Where you get justice without guile
> And Law without delay. (1774)

The inevitable Queen Victoria is also there, supported by putti who are not merely winged but fish-tailed too, ready for any eventuality. Higher still are Hercules in his lionskin, two caryatides, and quantities of women's heads in roundels to either side (one blindfold). At ground floor level, Justice is to the left, a toga'd lawgiver (Solon?) on the right, holding what should be a tablet or scroll, but is an anachronistic book. The angled archway has a boisterous frieze which includes eagles and swans.

THE MIDDLE TEMPLE occupies the area to the left (west) of Middle Temple Lane, but also has a number of buildings to the right (east). There was no geographical division of property between it and the Inner Temple until 1732. This is why the badges of the two Inns are so much in evidence, identifying which building belongs to which. After the order of Knights Templar

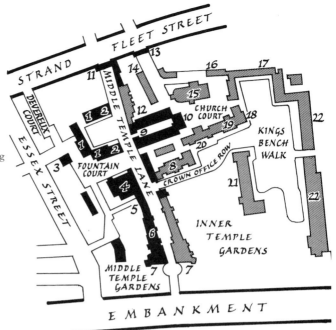

was dissolved in the early fourteenth century (see p. 93 for their history) another military holy order, the Knights Hospitaller, acquired their London headquarters and, at some point shortly after, bands of lawyers became their tenants. Shakespeare has it in *Henry VI* that in the following century the gardens here were the scene of the start of the Wars of the Roses. Richard Plantagenet, later Duke of York, suggests to the quarrelling magnates that, since no one is prepared to speak his mind,

> Let him that is a true-born gentleman,
> And stands upon the honour of his birth,
> If he suppose that I have pleaded truth,
> From off this brier pluck a white rose with me.

To which John Beaufort, Earl of Somerset, for the House of Lancaster, retorts:

> Let him that is no coward nor no flatterer
> But dare maintain the party of the truth,
> Pluck a red rose from off this thorn with me.

Incidentally, the one, anonymous, lawyer present chooses a white rose.

Sir Amias Paulet, Treasurer of the Middle Temple in the 1520s, had been unwise enough to cross the future Cardinal Wolsey when the latter was a young man. According to John Aubrey, Wolsey had committed 'some debauchery (I thinke, drunke: no doubt he was of a high rough spirit) and spake derogatorily of Sir Amias Paulet who put him in the stockes, which, when he came to be Cardinall, he did not forget; he laid a fine upon Sir Amias to build the Gate of Middle Temple.' A later sixteenth-century Treasurer of the Middle Temple, Edmund Plowden, is owed a great debt of gratitude by the Inn because it is he who was responsible for the building of its Hall. Regarded as the greatest and most honest lawyer of his age, he is supposed never to have left the Temple precincts for three years whilst studying for the Bar. When he died in 1584 he was buried in the Temple Church, in spite of being a Roman Catholic. He lives on in the phrase ' The case is altered', which owes its origin to a trial in which he was defending someone accused of (illegally) hearing mass. When it was revealed that the priest saying the mass was in fact a layman *agent provocateur*, Plowden was quickly on his feet: 'The case is altered: no priest, no mass.'

Opposite the effigy of Plowden in the Temple Church (p. 94) is another, slightly later one of Richard Martin: in John Aubrey's words, 'a very handsome man, a graceful speaker, facetious, and well-beloved. I think he dyed of a merry Symposiaque [drinking party] with his fellow-witts. He was Recorder [of London] but a moneth before his death [in 1618].' More than once his facetiousness got the better of him: in 1591 he was temporarily expelled from Middle Temple for rioting during the prohibited festival of the Lord of Misrule at Christmastide. In 1597 at dinner in Hall, John Davies, later Lord Chief Justice, was so provoked by Martin's rude criticism of one of his sonnets, that he attacked him with a cudgel.

A natural sequel to the Dissolution of the Monasteries by Henry VIII in 1536 was the abolition of the religious orders that had owned them. Thus the Temple had passed from the Hospitallers to the Crown in 1540 and the lawyers became its tenants, until James I granted them the freehold in 1609. Since the charter containing the grant is common to both Inns, it is housed on neutral ground, under the altar in the Temple Church. In 1613 the Middle and Inner Temple must have been keen to show their gratitude when participants in the masquing to celebrate the marriage of James's daughter Elizabeth to her German husband, the 'Palsgrave'. In 1634 their eldest son, Charles Louis, brother to the Cavalier commander Prince Rupert, was entertained at the Middle Temple by the *Masque of the Prince d'Amour*. This, the last formal masque to be mounted by an Inn, was attended by Charles I's queen Henrietta Maria, incognita in citizen's dress.

In Charles II's reign Francis North, later Lord Chancellor Guilford, was perhaps the most distinguished bencher of the Middle Temple. His younger brother Roger, also a bencher of the Middle Temple, has left a vivid portrait of him. He was a great believer in the value for a lawyer of much practical training and testing in the business of verbally setting forth an argument – something still very much part of today's training. As a student

he used constantly the commons in the hall at noons and nights [eating dinner and supper], and fell into the way of putting cases, which much improved him . . . He used to say that no man could be a good lawyer that was not a put-case. Reading goes off with some cloud, but discourse makes all notions limpid and just . . . [later] If he had no appointed company, he hath often taken me to walk about in the gardens with him till bed-time; for he never loved at such times to be alone; but, having any company, he could discharge his thoughts by discourse. After he was of the King's Counsel [a KC] he kept a coach and at leisure times used to air himself in that; but with a friend to receive his discourse and give handles for more . . . When he was made Attorney-General, though his gains by his office were great, they were much greater by his practice; for that flowed in upon him like an orage [storm], enough to overset one that had not an extraordinary readiness in business. His skull-caps . . . were now destined to lie in a drawer to receive the money that come in by fees. One had the gold, another the crowns and half-crowns, and another the smaller money. When these vessels were full they were committed to his friend [R. North] . . . to put it into large bags . . . and so they went to his treasurers, Blanchard and Child, goldsmiths at Temple Bar. [Child's branch of the Royal Bank of Scotland is still on the same spot.]

Left: A Jacobethan doorway to the Middle Temple Library
Right:Fountain Court, Middle Temple

Oliver Goldsmith, although no lawyer, lived in Brick Court from 1765 until his death in 1774, when he was buried somewhere to the north of the Temple Church. While resident he wrote, among much else, his play *She Stoops To Conquer*, and managed to disturb with his noise the great jurist Sir William Blackstone who had chambers below him. A little earlier, in 1763, the poet William Cowper, who was a member of the Inn, tried repeatedly and unsuccessfully to kill himself whilst living in the Temple, first with laudanum, then with a penknife and lastly by hanging himself with one of his garters. He was quite unfitted to the law, and when he heard that what seemed his only avenue of escape – to become a clerk in the House of Lords – involved an examination by the House, he could not face it. We must be profoundly grateful for his incompetence.

After you have come through the arch of Temple Gardens Building, as you advance up the slope past Middle Temple Library and Treasury on your left, the first building of note is **Middle Temple Hall**, which forms the south side of **Fountain Court**. It was completed about 1570 and it is thought that its double-hammerbeam roof was constructed by a carpenter who had been working at the great mansion of Longleat in Wiltshire, then being built by Sir John Thynne. The other ostentatious Elizabethan element is the screen, the doors of which were added in 1671. A bomb falling to the east of Middle Temple Lane in the last war blew in the east window of the Hall and reduced the screen to fragments, but these were collected and reconstructed. The bench table on the dais, twenty-nine feet long, is made from oak from Windsor Great Park floated down the Thames, the gift of Queen Elizabeth I. Below the dais, the smaller table called the cup-board is made from the timbers of the *Golden Hind*, the ship in which Drake, a member of the Inn, sailed round the world. In February 1602 Shakespeare's company performed *Twelfth Night* here, and who could be such a killjoy as to imagine that he wasn't either performing himself, or behind the scenes somewhere?

If you go a little higher up Middle Temple Lane from the Hall and then turn right, you should with luck find yourself in **Pump Court**. If you do not, do not worry: the best way to enjoy the Temple is to get a bit lost. In 1678 a fire began in Pump Court which burnt a large number of Temple buildings that had escaped the Great Fire of London in 1666. Roger North described how the young Duke of Monmouth, one of Charles II's bastards, 'who was setting up to be popular', came to help and superintend the blowing up of houses to stop the fire. 'I told the Duke if he thought it for the public service to blow up there [where Roger North's own chamber was] he was free to do it; and going out I heard him say he never met with people so willing to be blown up as these lawyers. So the train took, and my affair was at an end.' Except for the south side, Pump Court is as rebuilt in 1686. The magistrate and novelist Henry Fielding lived at number 4. Beyond Pump Court are the Tuscan-columned **Cloisters**, a post-war reconstruction of those built by Wren which in turn replaced the original Medieval cloisters. After 1678 the Middle Temple had wanted to build chambers instead, but the Inner Temple valued the cloisters as a place where 'students walking in the evening' could put cases to each other. Do they still?

Back in Middle Temple Lane, numbers 1, 2 and 3 at the top on the right are of 1693, a post-fire rebuilding but, with their timber frame and plaster construction, here they are still cocking a snook at the new regulations by then in place. On the left-hand (west) side of the Lane the last court is **Brick Court**. Go through the arch to the west and it will bring you to **New Court** and the gateway last seen when passing the Devereux pub (p. 78). This is a good point to say more about **NICHOLAS BARBON**, who has already been mentioned several times, because of his development of Red Lion Square, Bedford Row and Essex Street. The New Court block and gateway (1676) are also his work. Roger North knew him well because he did a lot of the rebuilding after the Middle Temple fire of 1678, and in his portrait of Barbon we recognise the archetype of the 'spec' builder and property developer.

His father, Praise God Barebones, was a leatherworker and a notorious Puritan fanatic (actually christened Unless-Jesus-Christ-had-died-for-thee-thou-hadst-been-damned), after whom Cromwell's Little Parliament of 1653 was named. Cromwell selected the members of this from 'godly men'. Of Nicholas Barbon, Roger North says:

Bred a doctor of physic, but that trade failing, he fell into that of building, and the fire of London gave him means of doing and knowing much of that kind . . . He was an exquisite mob master, and knew the arts of leading, winding, or driving mankind in herds . . . He was the inventor of this new method of building by casting of ground into streets and small houses, and to augment their number with as little front as possible, and selling the ground to workmen by so much per foot front, and what he could not sell, build himself . . . He said his trade would not afford to borrow . . . so he was forced to take the other way of being in debt . . . His way was to put men off from time to time by fair words [and if taken to court, to delay things as long as possible there. At meetings of those whose property he wanted to buy for development he took care to be] as richly dressed as a lord of the bedchamber on a birthday. [If any did not succumb to this] the first thing he did was to pull down their houses about their ears, and build upon their ground, and stand it out at law till their hearts ached, and at last they would truckle and take any terms for peace and a quiet life.

Although he became an MP and at one stage owned Osterley House outside London, Barbon eventually overreached himself and died in 1698. His genius may have been misapplied as a jerry-builder and developer, but he was also a pioneer of fire insurance and his *Discourse of Trade* (1690) displayed a remarkable grasp of economic theory for its time. It is unsurprising that Roger North saw through Barbon because he was himself no mean amateur of architecture – and music too. The **Gatehouse** at the Fleet Street end of Middle Temple Lane was designed by him (1684).

You can end the walk either by going up Chancery Lane to its eponymous tube, or back to the Temple tube. If you wish to go on to the Temple Church and the Inner Temple, turn right after passing under Middle Temple gateway and walk a short distance along Fleet Street before diving down Inner Temple Lane.

Numbers 1, 2 and 3 Middle Temple Lane, defying seventeenth-century building regulations

The Inner Temple and Fleet Street

Assuming that you have alighted at Chancery Lane tube and walked south down the Lane, you will be confronted at its end by the narrow but enticing frontage of **Simmonds' Bookshop** at number 16 Fleet Street. At this same address the eighteenth-century publisher and bookseller Bernard Lintot made a fortune for himself and for the poet Alexander Pope when he published Pope's verse translation of Homer.

On the other side of the archway leading to Inner Temple Lane is a staircase that will take you up to the splendid half-timbered building above, **Prince Henry's Room** (open Mon–Sat, 11 to 2, free). The prince in question was the elder brother of Charles I, and he predeceased their father James I. The premises were built in 1611 as a tavern called the Prince's Arms, which is exactly what is depicted in the contemporary plaster ceiling of the Room – the

Prince Henry's Room,
Fleet Street, above the entry
to Inner Temple Lane

A doorway, King's Bench Walk,
Inner Temple

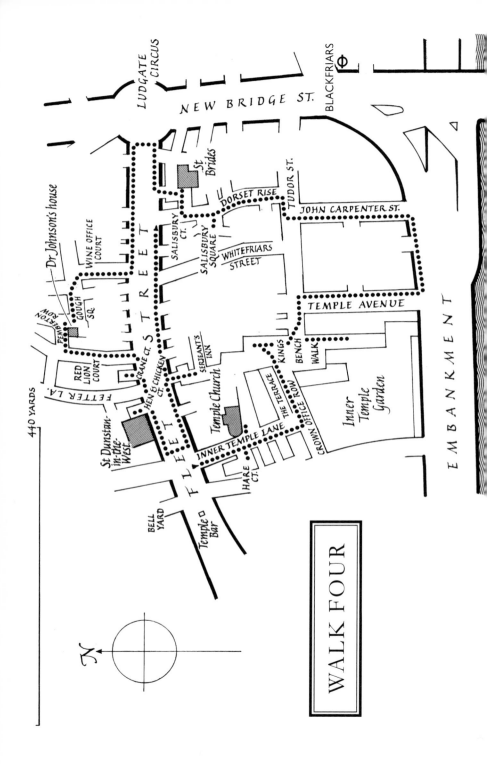

LUDGATE CIRCUS

NEW BRIDGE ST.

BLACKFRIARS

St Brides

DORSET RISE

JOHN CARPENTER ST.

Dr Johnson's house

WINE OFFICE COURT

SALISBURY CT.

SALISBURY SQUARE

WHITEFRIARS STREET

TUDOR ST.

PEWTERTON ROW

GOUGH SQ.

RED LION COURT

FETTER LA.

CRANE CT.

HEN & CHICKEN CT.

SERJEANT'S INN

S T R E E T

TEMPLE AVENUE

KINGS BENCH WALK

THE TERRACE

CROWN OFFICE ROW

Temple Church

Inner Temple Garden

E M B A N K M E N T

St Dunstan-in-the-West

F L E E T

INNER TEMPLE LANE

HARE CT.

BELL YARD

Temple Bar

440 YARDS

N

WALK FOUR

Three Feathers with the initials P H. There is one wall of good Jacobean oak panelling, while the rest is Georgian. The exterior was restored in the 1900s, when the bow windows were recreated. There is an exhibition of mementos connected with the diarist Samuel Pepys in the Room, and a good view up Chancery Lane from it.

Before perambulating the Inner Temple, now is the point to look at the **TEMPLE CHURCH**, which is common to it and to the Middle Temple. The order of Knights Templar was founded by a French and a Burgundian knight in 1118, in the Latin kingdom of Jerusalem established in Palestine after the success of the First Crusade. Its original title was 'Pauperes Commilitones Christi et Templi Solomoni' – the Poor Fellow-Soldiers of Christ and of the Temple of Solomon, a church in Jerusalem so called. The duty of these 'military monks' was to defend the Holy Land and protect the numerous pilgrims there; in return they were granted great privileges. Their admission rites and their chapter meetings remained secret, and they were answerable to the Pope alone. By about 1250 it was said they owned some 9000 manors all over Europe and the riches continued to flow into their treasuries because it was a lot less trouble to fulfil a crusading vow by paying them to fight on your behalf, than by setting out for Palestine yourself. The English kings certainly used what were in effect the banking facilities of the London Temple.

The fall of Acre in 1291 led to the evacuation of the Holy Land and the relocation of the Templars and Hospitallers in Cyprus. The Templars were now very vulnerable, because of their wealth and their loss of role , and in 1307 Philip IV of France, with a sub-servient French Pope, Clement V, in his pocket, began the attack on them. In true Stalinist style every kind of wild charge was thrown at them – idolatry, heresy, sodomy. If John Aubrey is to be believed, this last was an improbable one as far as London was concerned: 'the Knights Templars were notable wenchers, for whose convenience and use these stewes (next the Bear-Garden) on the Bankside [the south side of the Thames] were erected and constituted.' But this did not prevent the Templars' suppression in England by Edward II in 1312.

When building their churches, the Templars took as their model

Temple Church: the choir and one of the knights in the round nave

that of the Holy Sepulchre in Jerusalem, and so made them round. The nave of the Temple Church (not a parish church but a 'Royal Peculiar' like Westminster Abbey), though it may look like a castellated jelly-mould from the outside, is London's earliest Gothic (1160–85), its piers made up of two thicker and two thinner shafts through which daylight can be seen. The rectangular choir extending eastwards from it is a wonderfully serene example of thirteenth-century proportion (1220–40), aided and abetted by the harmonies of the grey Purbeck marble columns, the stone ribs, the off-white vaulting and the gold bosses. The fact that virtually everything you see is a post-Blitz restoration matters not one whit. One exception to this is the reredos, designed by Wren in 1682 and carved with peapods, sunflowers and ears of corn. It survived the bombing because it had been demoted by the Victorians and removed to the Bowes Museum at Barnard Castle. Notice also the unknown thirteenth-century bishop's effigy in the south aisle.

Returning to the round nave you pass the monuments to

Edmund Plowden and Richard Martin (p. 84), the former 'turning his toes to heaven', whilst the latter kneels. Plowden's Latin epitaph translates: 'I have lived amongst the billows; I die in safe haven.' But what are the two ladies in gold head-dresses and green wimples up to on either side? On the nave floor are the much defaced and restored effigies of eight knights, among them William Marshall, 1st Earl of Pembroke and two of his sons, the 2nd and 4th Earls. The 1st Earl (d. 1219) was a model of chivalry and of loyalty to his monarchs, ensuring the succession from King John to the young Henry III. Just before his death he assumed the habit of a Templar. Gilbert, the 4th Earl, died in 1241 after being dragged by his horse in a tournament. His body appears to be awkwardly twisted, his sword half-drawn, as indeed are some of the others'. They wear 'pot' helmets and chain mail, with big shields, though one exception is Robert de Ros (d. 1227). He is bare-headed and while his hands are in mail mittens, his mail head cover is gathered round his neck like a loose cowl. His shield bears his arms, three water-budgets – leather bottles. He opposed King John at the time of Magna Carta (1215) and left lands to the Templars. When you emerge from the church, look at the portal and porch at the west end, the eroded late seventeenth-century monument to the north and, beyond it, the Master's House, a post-war copy of the 1667 original. Master is the name given to the church's incumbent.

Whilst the Middle Temple may be proud of its performance of *Twelfth Night* (p. 87), the **INNER TEMPLE** has literary claims of its own. Geoffrey Chaucer is reputed to have been an early member, and to have been fined two shillings for beating a Franciscan friar in Fleet Street. In 1561, by coincidence on Twelfth Night, *Gorboduc* was performed before the young Queen Elizabeth. It is regarded as the first of English blank-verse tragedies and was written by two members of the Inner Temple, Thomas Norton and Thomas Sackville. In 1566 the queen gave her cousin Sackville the house and estate of Knole in Kent, which gift he was to pay for with his later years of service, ending as Lord Treasurer. He became the 1st Earl of Dorset and was the ancestor of the writer Vita Sackville-West, whose verdict on *Gorboduc* was that it is too gloomy and crude to be read now, except as a labour of love. From 1930 to 1945 number 4 King's Bench Walk, Inner Temple, was the

London address of V. Sackville-West and her husband Harold
Nicolson.

In 1572 the future Chief Justice Sir Edward Coke entered the
Inner Temple. As Attorney-General and Speaker of the House of
Commons, there was no more loyal servant of the Crown. For
instance he prosecuted Essex, Raleigh and the Gunpowder Plotters with rigour. But once made Chief Justice of the Common
Pleas in 1606, he led the opposition to any extension of the royal
prerogative or to the erosion of the independence of judges. It lost
him his position in 1616, but he continued his opposition as an
MP. His influence among lawyers also continued long after his
death in 1634, thanks to his commentary on an earlier fifteenth-
century Inner Templar's book on the subject of tenure. 'Coke on
Littleton' became the great authority on English real property law.
Aubrey says he was 'so fulsomely Pedantique that a schoole boy
would nauseate it. But when he comes to matter of Lawe, all
acknowledge him to be admirable.'

Another distinguished, but unswerving, servant of the Crown
in the seventeenth century, Thomas Wentworth, Lord Strafford,
was also of the Inner Temple. His master Charles I was unable to
save him from the scaffold in 1641. In 1683 there was something of
a reversal of circumstances, when Charles II was determined to
secure the execution of the republican Algernon Sidney, implicated like Lord William Russell (p. 39) in the supposed Rye House
Plot to kill the king. His tool was George Jeffreys of the Inner
Temple, called to the Bar when he was only 20, whose unscrupu-
lous bullying ways were just what was required. Charles at first did
hesitate, saying Jeffreys had 'no learning, no sense, no manners,
and more impudence than ten carted whores', but before long he
was leap-frogged into the position of Lord Chief Justice of the
King's Bench, and the king got the verdict he wanted. Jeffreys of
course cemented his reputation by his brutality in the Bloody
Assizes following the Duke of Monmouth's rebellion against
James II two years later.

In the eighteenth century Lord Chancellor Thurlow was of the
Inner Temple, after starting his training with William Cowper the
poet in the offices of a solicitor in Ely Place. William Hickey, that
lively Georgian rake and memoirist, recalled how hard it was to

track down Thurlow in the evening, 'by no means a laborious man in general, especially during the early part of his life'. He made a habit of never dining two successive days at the same tavern 'to avoid being interrupted in his hours of recreation by attorneys or their clerks'. Once, when sent by his attorney father to get an opinion from Thurlow, Hickey managed to extract his where-abouts from Thurlow's '*chère amie* the barmaid at Nando's'. Hickey went to the tavern she mentioned, where 'the host was inflexible, and would not peach, but in a few minutes after I entered, he called out: "Charles, carry up half a dozen of red sealed port into No. 3." It instantly struck me that must be the apartment my man was in.' Hickey was right, and so got his opinion.

As you walk down Inner Temple Lane towards the Temple Church, a block called **Dr Johnson's Buildings** is on the right. When James Boswell came to see Johnson for the second time, in 1763, it was at his chambers on this site, where he lived 'in literary state, very solemn and very slovenly'. One has to admire the perse-verance and nerve shown by Boswell, because when he had been introduced to Johnson for the first time, he was unwise enough to say, 'I come from Scotland, but I cannot help it'. Johnson retorted 'Sir, that, I find, is what a great many of your countrymen cannot help.' Later in the conversation Boswell presumed to know the actor Garrick's mind on some matter. 'Sir,' said Johnson, 'I have known David Garrick longer than you have done, and I know no right you have to talk to me on the subject.'

Johnson's friend Topham Beauclerk took Madame de Bouf-flers, mistress of the Prince de Conti, to see him here. When they had left, Johnson suddenly decided he should himself have shown the lady out. 'He overtook us before the Temple Gate, and, brush-ing in between me and Madame de Boufflers, seized her hand and conducted her to her coach. His dress was a rusty-brown morning suit, a pair of old shoes by way of slippers, etc. A considerable crowd of people gathered round and were not a little struck at his singular appearance.'

If you look at the list of barristers painted up by the door to Dr Johnson's Buildings you will see the name of John Mortimer QC, creator of that beloved character, **Horace Rumpole**. Portrayed by Leo McKern, he has delighted huge television audiences and

A sculpture of wrestlers in the gardens of Inner Temple, known to its inhabitants as 'the buggers'

Temple Gardens Building across Inner Temple Lawn

continues to win new followers in the books of short stories recounting his cases. Rumpole is a criminal lawyer, an Old Bailey hack, and proud of it. He has a wife called Hilda, or more often 'She Who Must Be Obeyed', 'a mind full of old murders, legal anecdotes and memorable fragments of the *Oxford Book of English Verse*, together with a dependable knowledge of bloodstains, blood groups, fingerprints, and forgery by typewriter.' He refers fondly to the great cases of his youth, the 'Penge Bungalow Murder' and the 'Peckham Billiard Hall Stabbing'. He chain smokes small cigars, wears a dirty old mac, and likes to drink dubious claret, which he calls Chateau Thames Embankment, in Pommeroy's wine bar. One feels he and Johnson would have seen eye to eye.

Behind Johnson's Buildings is **Hare Court** where Jeffreys had chambers. Charles Lamb, who lived at 4 Inner Temple Lane with his sister Mary from 1809 to 1817, called it 'a gloomy churchyard-like court with three trees and a pump in it . . . the water of which is excellent – cold with brandy, and not very insipid without it.' The centre of the Inner Temple suffered badly from bombing and as you walk southwards past the church and the cloisters you will see much rather uninspired post-war rebuilding. Find your way to the terrace between **Crown Office Row**, where Charles Lamb was born in 1775, the son of a clerk to one of the benchers, and the **Inner Temple Gardens**, where the annual show of the Royal Horticultural Society used to be held before it moved to Chelsea in 1913.

In an essay, Charles Lamb recalled how the 'Old Benchers of the Inner Temple' used to parade here in his childhood:

Coventry – whose person was a quadrate, his step massy and elephantine, his face square like a lion's, his gait peremptory and path-keeping, indivertible from his way as a moving column, the scarecrow of his inferiors, the brow-beater of equals and superiors, who made a solitude of children wherever he came, for they fled his insufferable presence . . . Clouds of snuff, aggravating the natural terrors of his speech, broke from each majestic nostril, darkening the air. He took it, not by pinches, but a palmful at once, diving for it under the mighty flaps of his old-fashioned waistcoat pocket.

At the east end of the terrace is **Paper Buildings**, so called because the original Jacobean structure was timber-framed, lath-and-plaster. But this was replaced by Sir Robert Smirke's present building in 1838. In the 1900s the Prime Minister's son Raymond Asquith, one of the most brilliant of the golden generation killed in the Great War, was training for the Bar here, and often overcome with melancholy: 'The window panes are covered with the dung of London pigeons, and from the room above I can sometimes hear the clerks spitting on the pavement.' Beyond it is **King's Bench Walk**, the most appealing part of the Inner Temple and so, like New Square at Lincoln's Inn, inevitably destined to be filled with cars. Many of the houses were designed by Wren (1678), but number 8 is of 1782 and 9 to 11 are of 1814. Turn your back on the car park and wander down their length comparing doorways, on which the decoration is concentrated.

Leave the Inn by its eastern gateway in the middle of King's Bench Walk and then turn right down Temple Avenue. You will not miss the alarming figures flanking a doorway halfway down.

Alarming figures in Temple Avenue
George and the Serpent, by Michael Sandle, in Dorset Rise

At a guess they are an Anglo-Saxon king with battleaxe and a chained captive. Then left, eastwards along the Embankment to **Sion College** (1886), home to a society for Anglican City clergy, originally founded elsewhere in 1624. Its redbrick Tudor Gothic by Sir Arthur Blomfield makes an interesting juxtaposition with the former **City of London School for Boys** (1882) on the other side of John Carpenter Street, all showy columns and those statues of Great Men, so often resorted to by the Victorians when they wanted to reassure themselves about their own place in history. It seems better suited to its new temple-of-mammon role, housing the J. P. Morgan Bank's London headquarters. This now stretches back down John Carpenter Street in a new building mirrored by its twin on the other side of the street. They look like post-modern versions of forbidding Florentine banker-princes' semi-fortified palazzos, with rustication up to the second floor and overhanging walkways and rails above. The facade of the old **Guildhall School of Music** (1887) has, however, been preserved. There are no statues, but the governors could not resist incising the great names

Sion College (left) and the City of London School for Boys (right) on the Embankment

of English music here instead. John Carpenter was Town Clerk of London in the early fifteenth century.

Continue north up Dorset Rise, past a new statue of St George slaying the dragon. The horse's head is stylized like a chess-piece, and the animal topples forward as the saint thrusts his lance down with both hands. The whole group seems to owe something to Tenniel's illustration of the White Knight in *Alice*. This street is at the centre of an estate, stretching from Fleet Street to the river and from New Bridge Street to Whitefriars Street, which Sir Richard Sackville (father of Thomas, Earl of Dorset, and of the Inner Temple) bought for £641 in 1564. It had belonged to the bishops of Salisbury, hence **Salisbury Square** at the top of the slope. Here Samuel Pepys was born in 1633, John Dryden lived in the 1670s, and Samuel Richardson, author of the interminable *Clarissa*, ran his printing business. The only original house is number 1, and that has been completely rebuilt. It is the home of that toothless organisation, the **Press Complaints Commission**, and must continually echo to the sound of doors shutting long after tabloid editors have bolted with yet another dingy scoop.

The Punch Tavern

Lutyens's main entrance to Reuters and the Press Association in Fleet Street, inverted obelisks either side of the door and Fame above

Next to it, on the east side of **Salisbury Court**, are virtually the only other survivors from the relocation of central London's last great manufacturing industry, **Reuters and the Press Association** in their 1935 Lutyens building. Its main frontage is on Fleet Street. Number 4/7 Salisbury Court is a Queen Anne-style building from 1878, with bow windows and plaster sunflowers below, that looks as though it has strayed from Bedford Park.

Just beside Lutyens' decorative inverted obelisks in Salisbury Court, go down the tunnel, St Bride's Avenue, which frames at its end the west doorway of Wren's church of **St Bride's** (1678). Above, out of sight, is the famous spire, the highest of all by Wren (1703), its five octagonal stages extended like some giant telescope down which the Almighty can peer at us, and no doubt find us wanting. The church was gutted during the War and then lavishly restored thanks to the munificence of the newspaper industry, but it was surely an error to have the woodwork in quite that shade of ginger. When the crypt was excavated, remains of a Roman build-

The swank of the old Daily Telegraph building

Wren's 'wedding cake' spire, St Bride's

ing (including a mosaic floor) and of a Saxon, a Norman and a later medieval church were found. You can see them, a patent cast-iron coffin, and also an exhibition on the history of printing in England.

Just to the north of St Bride's is the back door of the **Old Bell**, which claims to have been built by Wren for the refreshment of the men working on the church, and certainly has the feel of an eighteenth-century interior to it. Emerge from it into Fleet Street and have a look at its neighbour, number 92, **St Bartholomew House** (1900), a quality piece of Arts and Crafts work. There is a striking frieze of stone pomegranates and, at the top, recessed windows with short columns in front, all held up by a row of angels. If you haven't had a drink in the Old Bell, or even if you have, there is another chance at the **Punch Tavern**, almost at the south-east end of Fleet Street, and full of late Victorian gusto. The vestibule is done out in coloured tiles and paintings of Mr and Mrs Punch bowing and curtseying. Once inside, look up at the acid-etched glass in the skylight or the plasterwork with snarling

monster heads concealed in its foliage. The bar has a marble top
and the walls seem to have acquired their ochre tinge from a
genuine kippering in tobacco smoke.

On **FLEET STREET, NORTH SIDE**, opposite the Punch
Tavern, is what was, in Victorian times, the headquarters of
Thomas Cook the travel agents, hence the cherubs with globes
and the frieze of exotic faces, including a feathered Red Indian and
a Chinaman, adorning its frontage. Returning westwards along
this side, until the 1970s you would have passed the entry to
Racquet Court, with one or two late seventeenth-century houses
surviving down it. But it has now vanished off the map. Next to
where it was is the curved modernist black glass of the old **Daily
Express Building**, looking grubby and dejected. Its hall is one of
the great Art Deco interiors. Let's hope it survives. Its neighbour,
the old **Daily Telegraph Building**, with its garish clock, tends to
get described as Egyptian Classical, though it could equally well
pass as Aztec Art Deco. The twin Mercurys above the door, setting off in opposite directions, now preside over the employees of
Crédit Agricole and Goldman Sachs – 'the world's most successful investment bank', according to the *Daily Telegraph*.

Number 143–144, **Queen of Scots House**, was damned by
Pevsner as 'tastelessly and mercilessly Gothic', but its crisp mock-
medieval stonework, elaborate barge boards, and statue of the
queen are surely not so to be deplored. Turn into **Wine Office
Court** for the **OLD CHESHIRE CHEESE**. How did it, and the
other one in Little Essex Street, come by their names? The standard cheese consumed by Londoners in Tudor times was from
Suffolk but, as the market for butter grew, more and more of the
fat was skimmed off the milk for that before it went for cheese-
making. The Suffolk cheese grew hard; Pepys, for instance,
recorded 'my wife vexed at her people for grumbling to eat Suffolk
cheese.' At the end of the 1640s a cattle plague hit East Anglia,
which led to a shortage and a price rise. This stimulated the first
shipment of Cheshire cheese in the 1650s, twenty tons of it. So
popular did this superior product become that by the eighteenth
century, 7000 tons were coming in each year. It transformed Londoners' diets, and the Cheshire economy.

The tavern was rebuilt after the Great Fire in 1667. The

Dr Johnson's house in Gough Square and lunchtime in Wine Office Court

assumption is that such close neighbours as Dr Johnson and Oliver Goldsmith came here regularly. The only doubt has been raised by the discovery of some mid eighteenth-century pornographic tiles on the premises, which has led to the suggestion that it might have been a brothel and, as such, unlikely to have been patronized by the great moralist. It was famous for its steak-and-kidney puddings, each weighing over fifty pounds and with oysters, larks and mushrooms as added ingredients. The Victorian journalist George Augustus Sala evoked its glory days:

The waiters of the Cheese are always furious . . . How could it be otherwise when on the waiter's soul there lies the perpetual sense of injury caused by the savoury odour of steaks . . . of cheese bubbling in tiny tins; of floury potatoes and fragrant green peas; of cool salads, and cooler tankards of bitter beer . . . without being able to spare the time to consume them in comfort?

In the 1890s the Cheese was the meeting place for the group of poets called the Rhymers – Dowson, Yeats, Symons, Le Gallienne – full of *fin de siècle* decadence and delicate aesthetic sensibilities, yet choosing to come here to smoke long clay churchwarden pipes and drink beer out of pewter tankards.

Goldsmith lodged at 6 Wine Office Court from 1760 to 1763, trying to scrape a living as a hack writer. Finally his landlady appropriated his clothes, demanding either £36 arrears of rent or that he marry her. Johnson saved the day by bearing off the manuscript of *The Vicar of Wakefield* and selling it to a publisher for 60 guineas. In 1758 Johnson had borrowed 6 guineas from Samuel Richardson to avoid arrest for debt, so no wonder his sympathies were engaged. Goldsmith was a strange combination of vanity and generosity, adept at making himself look foolish. Joshua Reynolds' sister Frances claimed the effect of Goldsmith's bow on a roomful of people was to put them all at their ease, convinced they could not possibly make a worse one.

If you advance up Wine Office Court and swing to the left at the top, you will emerge into Gough Square where **DR JOHN-SON'S HOUSE** sits at the west end (open Mon to Sat, 11 to 5). Johnson is one of this area's tutelary spirits; he has already been encountered at Gray's Inn, Staple Inn, the Strand and the Inner Temple, but let him now be described by Boswell, fresh from his first meeting with 'the Great Cham' in May 1763:

Mr Johnson is a man of the most dreadful appearance. He is a very big man, and is troubled with sore eyes, the palsy, and the King's Evil [scrofula]. He is very slovenly in his dress and speaks with a most uncouth voice. Yet his great knowledge and strength of expression command vast respect and render him very excellent company. He has great humour and is a worthy man. But his dogmatic roughness of manners is disagreeable. I shall mark what I remember of his conversation.

He had arrived in London in 1737 with young David Garrick, his erstwhile pupil from his failed venture as a schoolmaster, the two of them sharing one horse. He could not have picked a worse moment to try and earn a living as a writer, since the traditional supports of governmental and noble patronage were vanishing and the great growth in the reading public was yet to come. After some years of journalism and hack work he extracted an advance payment from a consortium of booksellers and then moved into Gough Square to start compiling his great Dictionary. There lived with him various dependents; sometimes his wife Tetty, twenty-one years his senior and given to novel reading and the bottle; and, during working hours, the six assistants who copied out onto slips the 240,000 quotations marked by him in a host of books. From these, 114,000 were selected to support the 40,000 definitions in the finished work. It took nine years and when it appeared in 1755, it was a triumph, although written, as Johnson put it, 'not in the soft obscurities of retirement, or under the shelter of academick bowers, but amidst inconvenience and distraction, in sickness and in sorrow' (Tetty had died in 1752). For the sheer joy of rolling it off the pen, here is his definition of network: 'anything reticulated or decussated at equal distances with interstices between the inter-sections', and his reply to the lady from Plymouth who taxed him as to why he had defined 'pastern' wrongly: 'Ignorance, Madam, pure ignorance'.

The house is full of pictures and mementoes of him and his friends, though he might not have approved of the fitted carpet that has now been laid throughout. The most evocative room is the garret, at the top of the staircase whose banisters get cruder the higher it goes. Here he and his assistants worked, he in an elbow chair which he carefully propped against the wall, because it had only three legs. Look out for the brick from the Great Wall of China, which somebody gave him; for the hinged partition walls on the first floor, which allowed the two rooms and landing to be thrown into one for entertaining; for the massive chain across the front door.

When Johnson left the Inner Temple in 1765 he came back to live in Johnson's Court, and then moved to Bolt Court, both within spitting distance of here. He remained in Bolt Court from 1776 until his death in 1784. But nothing remains in either and you are better off going under the arch by Johnson's House (number 1 on its right is the only other original house left in the square), and then left a few yards along Pemberton Row, before turning into **Red Lion Court**. Number 18 is a fine late seventeenth-century house, formerly the premises of the distinguished 196-year-old scientific publishers, Taylor and Francis. There is a plaque on its wall of an oil lamp being refilled with the motto underneath: 'alere flammam' – keep the light burning.

Nor far from this place lyeth ye body of ye famd swordman ALEXANDER LAYTON Mr of defence ~ who departed this life ye 1st of June 1679

John Brewer of Grays Inn Esq (once a Scholl of his hath in Gratitude) caused this inscription to be made. 1681.

His Thrusts, like Lightning flew, more (Skilful Death Parried 'em all, and beat him out of (Breath

Hen and Chicken Court quietly rotting away, and a monument in St Dunstan-in-the-West

Surface briefly in Fleet Street before taking a look in to **Crane Court**, where both *Punch* and the *Illustrated London News* began their lives and the Royal Society used to meet before its palmy days in Somerset House. Nicholas Barbon rebuilt his father's house as numbers 5 and 6, after the Great Fire, but they were burnt out again in 1971. The slim cast-iron columns supporting round arches, proud of the windows, give number 2 a Venetian feel. Then across Fetter Lane, a quick look in to the spooky and decaying **Hen and Chicken Court** and past number 185, London home of those formidable Dundee publishers D. C. Thomson, among whose stable are not only the *Dundee Courier* and the *People's Friend,* as the building proudly tells you, but also *Beano* and *Dandy.*

The beguiling octagonal tower, fretted so it looks like the crown on some late-medieval statue of the Virgin, and the clock, the latter a lot older than the former, belong to **ST DUNSTAN-IN-THE-WEST**. The present church, in an assured if inauthentic picturesque Gothic by John Shaw, replaced an earlier one in 1833, at which point the 1671 clock went off to Regent's Park and was only brought back by Lord Rothermere in 1935. It is said to have been the first with two faces and the first with a minute hand in London. Two wild men hit bells above it with clubs to produce the chimes. (If you have children with you and they are growing fractious by this point, set them to counting the number of clocks projecting out into Fleet Street – there is a rash.) The exterior also boasts a statue of Queen Elizabeth (1586), given a home when Ludgate was demolished in 1760, and a bust of Lord Northcliffe (brother of Rothermere), sculpted by the widow of Scott of the Antarctic, Lady Hilton Young, as part of a memorial designed by Lutyens. The mythical King Lud and his sons, also from Ludgate, lurk inside the porch.

John Donne was rector of the previous church, though also Dean of St Paul's, whilst Izaak Walton, his biographer, was a member of the vestry. In 1667 Pepys was frustrated in his attempt to fondle 'a pretty, modest maid' here by her taking pins out of her pocket with which to prick him. The present interior, echoing the octagonal shape of the tower, is in need of some loving care, but do not dismiss it, for it houses some good memorials from its predecessor. In the side chapel next-but-one and to the right of the high altar, above a bench labelled 'free seats', is a plaque to: 'Ye Fam'd Swordsman, Alexander Layton, Master of Defence, d. 1679. His thrusts like light'ing flew/More skilful Death/Parried 'em all/And beat him out of breath.' A buttoned foil is carved either side of the inscription. Another reads, 'To the memory of Hobson Judkin Esq, late of Clifford's Inn, THE HONEST SOLICITOR, d. 1812'. The tablet was erected by his clients, so we must believe it. St Dunstan is the British centre for a number of other Churches, including the Rumanian Orthodox, hence the early nineteenth century iconostasis from Bucharest.

In 1847 the most successful of Victorian melodramas was first performed: *Sweeney Todd*, 'the demon barber of Fleet Street', whose shop was meant to be next to St Dunstan. Here his murdered victims disappeared through a trap door and were conveyed by a tunnel to Bell Yard where they were turned into mutton pies by an accomplice. Alas, there is no trace of an historical source for any

Some typical narrow Fleet Street frontages: in the left-hand picture the Cock Tavern is on the left and part of Gosling's Bank on the right. The picture on the right is of Number 29 Fleet Street. Pevsner called it 'perfectly horrible'. Shouldn't it rather be awarded marks for trying?

this, but it got a new lease of life from Stephen Sondheim's musical in 1979.

Number 187, next to St Dunstan and housing the TSB, is a very early example of Jacobethan (1834) by John Shaw junior, to complement his father's church. Next to that, until 1923, stood Praed's Bank, built by Soane in 1801. This area, particularly **FLEET STREET, SOUTH SIDE**, is suffused with banking history, though the only independent one left is **Hoare's Bank** at number 37. It is a dignified building in sandstone (1829) with the sign of the gilded leather bottle hanging outside. There are memorials to two Sir Richard Hoares (d. 1718 and 1754) in St Dunstan, both Lord Mayors. At number 19, Francis **Gosling's Bank** did business at the sign of the three squirrels in the eighteenth century. The present building is by Sir Arthur Blomfield (1899). Gosling had begun as a bookseller so such figures as Samuel Richardson and Edward Gibbon banked with him. **Child's Bank** at number 1 was founded in 1671, but the present building dates from 1879. Its sign is a marigold turning its face to the sun, with the motto 'Ainsi mon ame' – Thus my soul (turns to heaven). A marigold had been the sign of the inn on that site. If you look carefully at the facade you can pick out the marigold motif in several places. Dickens based the interior of Tellson's Bank in *A Tale of Two Cities* on the old Child's: 'the triumphant perfection of inconvenience'.

By treating the banks together, we have got slightly out of order on the south side of Fleet Street. The **Cock Tavern** at number 21 only dates from 1887; the original was on the north side. At number 32 (actually in the passage leading to Falcon Court) a plaque reminds that the publisher John Murray set up here in 1768, but the firm only got into its stride in the 1800s, publishing Walter Scott's poem *Marmion*, launching the Tory *Quarterly Review* as a riposte to the Whig *Edinburgh Review*, and Mrs Rundell's *Domestic Cookery*, the first cookbook aimed at the ordinary household rather than the professionals. Then along came Lord Byron with the first two cantos of *Childe Harold*. They were published in March 1812, and Byron 'awoke one morning and found myself famous'. They only sold 4500 copies in six months but that, and the annual sale of between 5000 and 10,000 of Mrs Rundell, were enough to finance the move to Albemarle Street in the West End, in pursuit of the fashionable world, where the firm still is.

El Vino at number 47 was the journalists' watering hole *par excellence* and a scene of various confrontations over its refusal to serve women at the bar, as opposed to the table. It is still haunted by the shade of Lunchtime O'Booze. The **Norwich Union** building at number 49 has a pleasant sculptural group (by Stanley Young, 1913) of blindfold Justice, a putto with cornucopia, and another female with shield and palm or olive branch. Turn in by it and you have entered **Serjeant's Inn** – or its site, because all is bland neo-Georgian now and the last Serjeant left long ago (see p. 117). It stretches down to Mitre Buildings, part of the Inner Temple. Back in Fleet Street, number 53 has an alarming frontage of green and plum diapered bricks, whilst number 56–7 has an Aztec or ziggurat-effect top, with friendly Scottish symbols below: thistles, snarling lions. In the seventeenth century, the area around Whitefriars Street was known as Alsatia and was a haunt of thieves and footpads. Hanging Sword Alley off it was earlier known as Blood Bowl Alley. Number 65 is the new offices of the solicitors Freshfields, all slick granite and glass. There are many such, full of thrusting foreign banks, law firms and accountants, colonising the territory left vacant by the departed newspapermen. But Fleet Street still offers a glorious architectural hodge-podge of narrow frontages on which to exercise the eye, even if one can no longer buy here the early editions at 11.30 p.m., and so get the smug satisfaction of being in the know before the rest of the nation. Blackfriars tube is the closest to take you home.

Peace and Justice – carved in 1913 – at number 49 Fleet Street

THE FIRST 250 YEARS

When lawyers first began living communally in the fourteenth century it was in the suburbs that they settled, around Holborn Bars and Temple Bar, the western boundary of the City of London. A few hundred yards to the east, the City walls were pierced at Ludgate and Newgate and roads emerged to cross the Fleet or Holbourne river by bridges before climbing westwards to the Bars. The southern one, Fleet Street, became the Strand at Temple Bar and then followed the Thames round southwards to Westminster, where the King's new centralised courts dispensed justice. Along it the lawyers could commute to their work, if they did not take a boat from Temple Stairs. This geographical location, equidistant from the power centres of the Royal Court at Westminster and the City's Guildhall, is symbolic of the independence and uniqueness of the Inns of Court. That great historian F. W. Maitland pointed out,

No English institutions are more distinctively English than the Inns of Court . . . unchartered, unprivileged, unendowed, without remembered founders . . . What is distinctive of medieval England is not Parliament, for we may everywhere see assemblies of Estates, nor trial by jury, for this was slowly suppressed in France; but the Inns of Court and the Year Books that were read therein, we shall hardly find their like elsewhere.

The first record is Lincoln's Inn's Black Book beginning in 1422, so there has been room for much speculation about the early days. The idea that the Inns were teaching institutions from the start has now been discarded; rather they were practical self-help assemblages of lawyers during term time, to ensure mutual protection, accommodation and communal eating. In this they resembled the halls at medieval Oxford and Cambridge before these were superseded by the more structured colleges. At some point in the fifteenth century the Inns widened their membership to take in unqualified youths and began to teach them law. It seems that from the very early days of this development, a large number of those entering the Inns were the sons of well-to-do fathers, sent for a few years because of the general educational opportunities afforded rather than to turn them into practising lawyers. In 1468, in his book *De Laudibus Legum Angliae* (In Praise of the Laws of England), Chief Justice Sir John Fortescue wrote, 'a student cannot well be maintained under eight and twenty pounds a year . . . For this reason the students are sons to persons of quality.' As well as the law, the youths could get tuition in dancing, music, fencing and other courtly arts from the tutors who clustered round the Inns.

As the medieval period gave way to the Tudor this new role for the Inns, as finishing schools for the sons of the nobility and gentry, became well established. The pattern was to go to them aged perhaps 17 or 18, after a few years at one of the Inns of Chancery (p. 116), or at Oxford or Cambridge. Whilst the young men were in the Capital, the Inns provided not only convenient lodgings but also a readymade network of acquaintances to cultivate. Whatever knowledge of law they managed to acquire would, as Sir Humphrey Gilbert said, help them 'to put their owne case in law, and to have some judgement in the office of a justice of the peace and sheriffe'. They could expect to hold these offices when they returned to their counties, as well as to be involved in lawsuits themselves in what was a very litigious age. Admissions, which had only been about sixty a year, were up to a hundred a year by 1550 and two hundred and fifty by 1600; the cost had gone up to £40 a year, but there were still no scholarships. Gray's Inn was by far the most prestigious at this time, though much building of gateways, halls, chapels and libraries was continuing at all of them. Sets of chambers were thrown up as speculations by private members; gardens were laid out.

In 1605 Ben Jonson dedicated his play *Every Man Out of His Humor* to 'the noblest nurseries of humanity and liberty, in the kingdome – the Innes of Court . . . I understand you, gentlemen, not your houses.' The members of the Inns provided an appreciative audience for the new drama being written by him, Shakespeare, Francis Beaumont of the Inner Temple, and their contemporaries – the theatres on Bankside were the shortest of boat trips away from Temple Stairs. If these playwrights had been able to look to Church and Court alone, previously the only sources of artistic patronage, it is impossible to imagine them achieving such range and depth.

The Inn members were not, however, content to be a mere passive audience for the literary and dramatic outburst of the Elizabethan and Jacobean age. Plays and masques were continually put on at the Inns; the writing of poetry seems to have become a consuming pastime for many there, reaching its apogee in the circle around John Donne of Lincoln's Inn, with their intricate, witty, hard-nosed verses. Masters of the Revels were appointed to lead the formal all-male dances round the Inn halls, which took place on every Saturday night between All Saints Day (November 1st) and Candlemas (February 1st). In the seventeenth century gambling took over from dancing as the chosen relaxation during this season. Inner Temple butlers earned most of their income by acting as croupiers at Christmastide, and when the floor boards of Middle Temple Hall were taken up in 1764, nearly 100 pairs of very small dice were found, which had fallen through the cracks. In part this, along with the drinking, wenching and elaborate dressing, was inspired by the desire to get as close to the manners and diversions of the Royal Court as possible. The sons of gentry at the Inns were bent on differentiating themselves from the professionals who looked to earn their living from the Law by actually practising as barristers, and whose status at this very time was not very high.

That said, the Law had, by Elizabeth's reign, usurped the Church as the best avenue of advancement for the bright boy from a modest background: 'whosoever studieth the laws of the realme . . . he shall be called master . . . and shall be taken for a gentleman'. Prosperity was spreading, but was accompanied by the complication of inflation; the land market was highly active, absorbing and redistributing the mass of property made available by the Dissolution of the Monasteries; commerce was expanding, and agriculture changing under the influence of the enclosure of the open fields. Barristers were deeply involved in all the consequent activity, not merely in the law courts, but also acting as land agents, accountants, brokers, financiers. Not only was there a dearth of professionals to call upon, apart from themselves, attorneys and solicitors, but the restrictions on and distinctions between these types of lawyer were not yet in place. In 1635, thirty-two members of the Middle Temple were practising as attorneys. Barristers could still deal directly with clients and drew up briefs and pleadings themselves, whilst attorneys still had the right of audience in the Westminster courts.

The right of audience, the right to be heard, was the bedrock on which the Inns of Court established their position and to which they still owe their prominence. Until he has been called to the Bar of his Inn, a barrister cannot be heard, cannot practise in the courts. One might have expected the judges to have controlled who could plead before them; instead it is the Inns, though of course the judges themselves are Inn members, normally benchers, as senior members are called. The accepted time to be spent as a student before being 'called' was seven years, and in the last two, attendance at between four and six 'learning vacations' was expected. The vacations were the periods between the four law terms each year. The courts at Westminster sat during the Hilary, Easter and Trinity terms, which lasted for three weeks each, and the Michaelmas one of four weeks.

The students were also required to have participated in a number of the 'moots' regularly arranged by their Inn. These mock trials were one of the three elements of the aural 'out loud' training (as distinct from book learning) for barristers. The other two were more informal 'case-putting' – the discussion of two or three questions of law – and 'readings'. Confusingly, these last were in fact formal lectures on some area of the law, which then served as the basis for disputations and discussions over several weeks following. For the rest, it was a matter of reading the year books and the reports of trials and making digests of them into your commonplace book.

THE INNS OF CHANCERY, ATTORNEYS AND SOLICITORS

How did the Inns of Chancery fit into the scheme of things? Their origins are about as ancient and obscure as those of the Inns of Court, but they never rose to such eminence, because they never had the power to bestow qualifications on lawyers. By the sixteenth century they were acting as out-stations of the Senior Inns, places where youths went for a short period before progressing to the latter. Staple and Barnard's were linked with Gray's; Furnival's and Thavies with Lincoln's; Clement's, Clifford's and Lyon's with the Inner Temple, New and Strand with the Middle Temple. By the seventeenth century these connections were withering as more and more students went straight to the Inns of Court. The Inns of Chancery were left to the attorneys and solicitors, who tended to be elbowed out of the Inns of Court by the barristers as the century wore on. Much of the public's time-honoured hatred of lawyers was now specifically channelled towards attorneys. Dr Johnson said of an acquaintance 'that he did not care to speak ill of any man behind his back, but he believed the gentleman was an attorney.'

Since 1875 the functions of solicitor and attorney have been merged, but originally the former practised in the chancery courts and was concerned with property work, whilst the latter practised in the common law courts. The Inns of Chancery never played the organising role for them that the Inns of Court played for the barristers; in the eighteenth century they were not much more than convivial clubs, and the foundation of the Law Society in 1825 as the professional body for attorneys and solicitors meant the end of them.

SERJEANTS-AT-LAW AND SILKS

Serjeants are another ingredient that has vanished from the legal scene. From the Middle Ages, only they could plead at the court of Common Bench (later called Common Pleas), which was the busiest and the most profitable. Only from their ranks could Common Law judges be chosen. They wore parti-coloured robes and a white linen coif or cap. A royal writ was needed to be appointed Serjeant, and once appointed, he ceased being a member of his old Inn of Court and joined one of the two Serjeants' Inns, at the south-east end of Chancery Lane, and between Fleet Street and the Inner Temple.

The means of their eclipse lay in the new rank of King's (or Queen's) Counsel – KCs or QCs – for senior barristers, created in 1605. (KCs or QCs are also known as 'silks', for such is the material from which their gowns are made, and when they are promoted to the rank they are said to have 'taken silk'.) It was in fact only in the nineteenth century, when the rank ceased to be a political appointment, that their numbers increased and they began to monopolise the benches of their Inns, of which they remained members, unlike Serjeants. In 1846 the Court of Common Pleas was opened to all members of the Bar and in 1875 the Serjeants were finally abolished.

THE NEXT 250 YEARS

The Inns did not escape the general disruption of life by the Civil War. The exercises of readings, moots, etc, were not performed at all between 1642 and 1647, and the educational system of which they formed part rapidly disintegrated as the century went on. The expensive feasting and present-giving expected of a reader made that an honour to be avoided. Francis North, Lord Guilford, spent £1000 when reader at the Middle Temple in 1671. Moots and case-putting were skipped or their motions merely gone through. To be elected to one's Inn's bench became a sign of success rather than of learning.

After 1680 admissions fell steeply, partly due to the expense, up to £100 a year now, and to the added burden of war taxation on the gentry; partly because the expanded army and civil service offered alternative careers to young men. There were still many 'non-professional' students, but the numbers actually qualifying as barristers were going up. On the other hand, the qualification had been devalued by the ending of exercises and by students being allowed to buy the right to qualify in three or four years rather than seven. Training now was a matter of reading and 'common-placing', perhaps taking up a clerkship with an attorney, or entering the chambers of a 'special pleader' to learn the arts of pleading, attending at Westminster Hall to gain familiarity with procedures and language (law French was only dropped in 1731), and un-official case-putting and moots with one's contemporaries.

The prosperity of the Inns was affected not only by falling

admissions, but also by a strengthening tendency towards non residence, both by practising barristers and by 'non-professionals'.
'Commons', the corporate catering provided in the halls, were not
used to the full, and members chose to live elsewhere than in
chambers. The financial loss was made up by relaxing the rules so
that non-members could reside, and run their businesses from
chambers, whether these were used as offices or in some cases
converted into shops. By 1733 there were twenty-two such in the
Middle Temple, including a barber, a hatter and a shoemaker. As
Roger North was to bemoan, the Inns 'have the outward show or
pretence of collegiate institutions, yet in reality, nothing of that
sort is now to be found in them.'

Whilst fees had increased greatly during the seventeenth century, the amount of litigation dropped considerably towards 1700,
and went on dropping thereafter. The division of labour between
barristers and attorneys or solicitors became more distinct and the
former ceased to do property conveyancing or to prepare briefs
after meetings with clients. These had been valuable sources of
income to newly qualified barristers and so it became even harder
to survive the early years before one had established a client base.
There was no easy living to be earned from the law, even though
such areas of business as insurance, banking and the stock market
were expanding. Barristers were not involved in criminal trials
until the late eighteenth century. It is difficult to arrive at an accu-
rate figure for those relying on the Bar for their living, but it has
been calculated that in 1785 it was at the minimum only 121, and
the maximum 295.

The numbers of admissions coming from a gentry background
declined and in 1762, in an attempt to stem the middle-class tide,
those with an Oxbridge degree were allowed to be called after
three years rather than the five that had become the norm. In
1825 all except Gray's, which could not afford to turn anyone
away, started requiring two character references, each signed by
two barristers.

The first stirring of reform was perhaps the County Courts Act
of 1846, which established this level of court and allowed attorneys right of audience in them. But the requirement of students
was still only to eat three dinners a term for twelve terms in hall,

and wait for between three and five years. Dickens, jaundiced as ever, defined it in *The Uncommercial Traveller* as 'having a frayed old gown put on, and, so decorated, bolting a bad dinner in a party of four, whereof each individual mistrusts the other three.' (One ate in hall in 'messes' of four.) In 1852 the Council of Legal Education was established, whose lectures had to be attended *or* an exam be passed, before one could be called to the Bar. In 1872 the exam became compulsory. As the nineteenth century progressed, the numbers qualifying increased greatly as did the members then managing to earn a living, but the latter as a percentage of the former decreased, which indicates that the Bar was getting ever more competitive. By 1885 the practising Bar could have been as small as 660 or as large as 1450. The opportunities for lawyers to find work in the Bars of the various British colonies, in the expanding home civil service and in business, luckily meant that much of the slack was taken in.

In the 1870s the Judicature Act saw the Courts of Common Pleas and the Exchequer being swallowed up by the King's Bench Division. In the early 1880s new rules of court procedure meant that much business was taken out of the hands of junior barristers and into solicitors'. This did prompt the formation of a Bar Committee, but it achieved little. Only its replacement in 1894 by the Bar Council saw the Inns at last confronting the need for some sort of united front. Discipline was left in the Inns' hands, but the Council could speak on etiquette and represent the Bar in dealings with Parliament, Ministers, Press and judges. In 1919 women were allowed to be called to the Bar.

THE PRESENT DAY

In the past few decades one of the greatest influences for change has been the growth of the legal aid system, which began in 1950 as part of the post-war welfare state legislation. Government funds administered by the Lord Chancellor pay for the legal expenses of the less well off. The injection of money has enabled recently qualified barristers to find work more easily and so they have not needed a private income to keep afloat during the difficult early days of their careers. However, the costs of the scheme have been running away in recent years and severe cuts were made in April 1993. Since the figure for 1994-5 is estimated at £1.4 billion, compared to £500 million for 1989, further cuts look to be in order. There is certainly a tendency now for the brightest graduates to go for the more guaranteed rewards of a solicitor's career.

Those entering the Inns of Court are all graduates, though ones from Oxbridge are very much a minority. Before being called, they must have dined eighteen times in the hall of their Inn, besides spending a year working for their Bar exams. Part of this work will have been a vocational course at the Inns of Court School of Law, including role-playing exercises not so very far removed from those performed by their sixteenth-century predecessors. After being called, they will have a year's 'pupillage' in a set of chambers: sitting in on conferences, going to court with their 'pupil master', looking up points of law for him or her. In the second six months they can take on work of their own, if they are lucky enough to be offered it. Attempts are being made to secure a minimum salary for this year of pupillage.

There is no guarantee, once your year is up, that you will be offered a 'seat' in that set of chambers, because there are too many aspirants for the number of places available. At the moment between forty and fifty per-cent of those called to the Bar are having to drop out within the first two years. The number of barristers has grown to over 7500, whilst there are over 60,000 solicitors.

The average set of chambers has seventeen members, with three or four often sharing a room. The pressure on space means that a number of chambers are now located outside the confines of the Inns themselves. Barristers remain self-employed and are not allowed to form themselves into partnerships. Neither can they be 'briefed' directly by members of the public (except now by certain professions such as accountants and surveyors). Contact with a client can only be via a solicitor, and the person in chambers who acts as the conduit from the firms of solicitors is the clerk. He is still a figure of great power, and often of wealth too; and it is at his whim whether the new member of chambers gets the odd brief coming his or her way. However, a recent reform does now allow a barrister to work from home and deal direct with solicitors after three years in chambers.

An added peril of the profession is that a barrister cannot sue for the non-payment of a fee, though the reverse of this is that neither can he be sued for non-appearance or negligence in court. Soon he will be allowed to work, like his American counterpart, on a no win, no fee basis. But his contingency fee (as it is called) if successful, will not be a percentage of the damages gained; rather it will be double the normal fee.

There are now about 860 Queen's Counsel, at the top end of the profession. Seventy-seven new ones were made in 1994 by the Lord Chancellor after consultation with senior officials, judges and barristers. This was only fifteen percent of those who applied to become QCs that year. Since 1977 they have not been obliged to have a junior barrister with them in court, but in practice they still nearly always do. The client thus not only pays the higher fees of the QC himself, but another set of fees for the junior too. There is no guarantee that a QC's services will be perceived to be worth the extra once he has taken silk, and clients could go elsewhere. But if he becomes in demand, then £200,000 p.a. is not unusual.

In 1993 the Lord Chancellor conducted a survey to see whether wigs should be retained. Many of the most senior judges wanted to see them go, but the majority of those polled (a mix of judges, barristers and the public) wanted to keep them. So a judge can still say that he 'cannot see' a barrister in court, should he be without gown, white bands under his chin, or wig on his head. The black gowns are said to be those adopted for mourning at the death of Charles II in 1685, and never discarded. The long, full-bottomed wig is only worn on ceremonial occasions by judges and QCs, and varieties of the short one are worn in court. They are made from the hair of horses' manes now, rather than human hair as was the case before 1834. In that year Humphrey Ravenscroft patented his new method, which got rid of the need to anoint the wig's curls regularly with pomade to stop them unrolling. It also made the wigs lighter and much more durable.

One of the other recent major reforms, under the Courts and Legal Services Act of 1990, is to give solicitors the right of audience in Crown Courts, the High Court, and the Appeal Courts. So since 1994 the solicitor-advocate has started to emerge on the scene and the barristers' monopoly is no more.

However, the dire prophesyings that a fusion of the two branches would immediately ensue do not seem likely to be ful- filled. The old lines of demarcation may have become blurred, and solicitors' firms may have grown in size, as has the level of special- isation they offer. But both branches were hit by the recent reces- sion and, while barristers felt the pinch from cuts in legal aid, solicitors suffered from the fall in the number of property deals, having already lost their lucrative monopoly of conveyancing in 1985. The Inns and the Bar look like surviving for some time yet.

INDEX

Italic numbers indicate illustrations